THE METABOLIC FLEXIBILITY COOKBOOK FOR BEGINNERS

Unlock Your Body's Fat Burning Potential and Fuel Your Weight Loss Journey with Delicious Recipes and Powerful Nutritional Strategies

BY
ELOISE HEWITT

TABLE OF CONTENT

INTRODUCTION

Welcome to "The Complete Metabolic Flexibility Cookbook," your one-stop shop for improving metabolic flexibility through delicious and nutritious meals. Metabolic flexibility refers to our bodies ability to switch between utilizing different energy sources, such as carbs and lipids, based on our energy needs. Achieving metabolic flexibility has been found to support stable blood sugar levels, promote weight loss, and reduce the risk of chronic diseases such as diabetes and heart disease. Obesity, insulin resistance, and diabetes are just a few of the health problems that can result from a lack of flexibility caused by unhealthy eating habits, inactivity, and other aspects of one's lifestyle.

Because it enables your body to utilize the available energy sources effectively, metabolic flexibility is an important concept for overall health and wellness. Your body can switch between using carbohydrates and fats as a fuel depending on what is available and what your body needs at any given time when you have good metabolic flexibility. This can promote weight loss and provide other health benefits in addition to preventing fluctuations in blood sugar levels and energy crashes.

This cookbook is intended to assist you in achieving metabolic flexibility through a well-balanced diet high in whole foods. There are recipes that are not only delicious but also help you increase your metabolic flexibility. This cookbook also includes information on the benefits of metabolic flexibility, the science behind it, and how to improve your metabolic flexibility.

This cookbook offers 150 delightful and nutritious recipes that are intended to advance metabolic flexibility and work on generally speaking wellbeing. Refined sugars, grains, and processed oils are not included in the recipes, which are based on whole, unprocessed foods. They offer suggestions for meal planning and preparation as well as a selection of breakfast, lunch, dinner, and snack options.

In addition to the recipes, the book provides useful advice on how to incorporate healthy habits into your daily life and useful information on the science behind metabolic flexibility. "The Complete Metabolic Flexibility Cookbook" is a useful resource for anyone interested in optimizing their health through diet and lifestyle choices. It can be used to improve metabolic health, lose weight, or just enjoy delicious and nutritious meals.

WHAT IS METABOLIC FLEXIBILITY?

Metabolic flexibility is the capability of the body to adjust to changes in energy demands and transition between using multiple fuel sources to generate energy, such as carbs, lipids, and ketones. It is an important part of metabolic health because it allows our bodies to maintain stable blood sugar, aid in losing weight, and eliminate the risk of chronic diseases.

When we eat carbs, our bodies use glucose as the primary fuel source, however, when we eat fats, our bodies use fatty acids as the primary fuel source. The body of a metabolically flexible person can efficiently switch between these diverse fuel sources dependent on the body's energy demands. For example, during exercise, the body may use carbs as the primary fuel source, whereas during fasting, the body may switch to fat as the primary fuel source.

Diet, exercise, sleep, and heredity are among the factors that can influence metabolic flexibility. A sedentary lifestyle and a diet high in processed foods and sugar can impair metabolic flexibility, whereas regular exercise and a balanced diet rich in whole foods can increase it.

Improving metabolic flexibility is important for general health and wellness and can be accomplished by lifestyle changes including diet and exercise. It is important to consult a healthcare professional to create a customized plan to improve your metabolic flexibility.

IMPROVING YOUR METABOLIC FLEXIBILITY

Changing one's lifestyle to make it easier for the body to switch between using different fuel sources like carbohydrates and fats is one way to increase metabolic flexibility. Here are some other effective ways to increase your metabolic flexibility:

Include HIIT (High-Intensity Interval Training) in Your Workout Schedule
HIIT is a type of exercise that alternates brief intense workouts with periods of rest or lower-intensity activity. Short, intense, and efficient, HIIT workouts typically last anywhere from 10 to 30 mins. HIIT has the potential to improve fat burning, muscle tone, and cardiovascular fitness. HIIT can produce comparable results to longer, steady-state workouts in a shorter amount of time, making it an efficient way to exercise. Instances of HIIT exercises incorporate running stretches, bouncing jacks, and burpees. HIIT can be altered to fit the wellness level of the individual, and it tends to be finished regardless of gear. To avoid injury, it is essential to properly warm up before beginning HIIT and to listen to your body. By increasing the body's capacity to use fat as fuel both during exercise and rest, this type of exercise has been shown to improve metabolic flexibility.

Boost Your Daily Activity Level
Casual work, like strolling or cycling, can work on Metabolic flexibility by expanding the body's muscles and further developing insulin sensitivity.

Eat a well-rounded diet
A well-balanced diet that includes a range of whole foods such as fruits, vegetables, lean protein, and healthy fats helps enhance metabolic flexibility by giving the body the nutrition it needs to function efficiently.

Intermittent fasting is a good idea
Intermittent fasting(IF) involves eating and fasting at different times. The most common way to practice intermittent fasting (IF) is to fast for a set number of hours each day or on specific days of the week. Irregular fasting enhances weight reduction, further developed insulin responsiveness, decreased inflammation, and further developed cognitive capability. Intermittent fasting may also help lower the danger of certain chronic diseases like cancer, diabetes, and heart disease, according to some studies. It is essential to keep in mind that intermittent fasting may not be suitable for everyone, particularly pregnant women and those with a history of eating disorders. To support your general health and well-being, it's also important to make sure you get enough calories and nutrients during

your eating periods. If you're thinking around trying intermittent fasting, it's a good idea to talk to a doctor first. This approach has been displayed to work on Metabolic flexibility by expanding the body's capacity to use fat as fuel during fasting periods.

Keep away from processed food and Sugar

Sugar and processed foods can mess up the body's natural metabolic processes, making it harder for the body to use fat as fuel and develop insulin resistance.

Get sufficient rest

Metabolic flexibility can be negatively impacted by insufficient or poor-quality sleep. Try to get 7 to 8 hours of good sleep each night.

Reduce Stress

When the body is metabolically rigid, it may be less efficient at utilizing glucose and fatty acids for energy, resulting in higher HPA axis stress. This can lead to elevated cortisol levels and a persistent stress response, both of which can be detrimental to general health and well-being. When the body is metabolically flexible, it can switch between using glucose and fatty acids for energy more efficiently, which may assist to alleviate stress on the HPA axis.

THE BENEFITS OF ACHIEVING METABOLIC FLEXIBILITY

There are numerous advantages to achieving metabolic flexibility for overall health and wellness. The following are a few advantages of achieving metabolic flexibility:

Stable Glucose Levels

To maintain stable blood sugar levels, metabolic flexibility enables the body to switch between using various fuel sources like carbohydrates and fats. This can lessen the gamble of creating type 2 diabetes and further develop energy levels.

Improved Weight Management

When the body's metabolism becomes more flexible, it becomes more adept at switching between using carbohydrates and fat as fuel sources. This can help the body control energy levels more effectively, lowering the risk of overeating and weight gain.

Enhancement of Athletic Performance

Metabolic flexibility can work on athletic execution by permitting the body to switch between involving sugars and fats as fuel during exercise, advancing perseverance and reducing weakness.

Greater levels of energy

Metabolic flexibility can boost energy levels and reduce fatigue by enhancing the body's capacity to utilize various fuel sources.

Enhanced Cognitive Capacity

There is a link between improved cognitive performance and metabolic flexibility.

Longevity

Accomplishing Metabolic flexibility has been related to expanded life expectancy and improved health span.

Enhanced Heart Health

By lowering inflammation and enhancing blood lipid profiles, metabolic flexibility can improve cardiovascular health.

Cancer Risk Reduction

Studies recommend that further developing Metabolic flexibility might decrease the gamble of particular kinds of disease, including bosom and colon malignant growth.

Better gut health
By encouraging the growth of healthy gut bacteria and reducing gut inflammation, metabolic flexibility may improve gut health.

Reduced Inflammation
Numerous chronic diseases have been linked to chronic inflammation, and increasing metabolic flexibility may reduce inflammation and improve health as a whole.

Enhanced Immune Performance
Metabolic flexibility might work on safe capability by advancing the development of insusceptible cells and reducing aggravation.

Better skin health
By reducing oxidative stress and inflammation, metabolic flexibility may improve skin health.

Lower Probability of Cognitive Decline
Improved cognitive function and a lower risk of cognitive decline have been linked to metabolic flexibility.

In conclusion, achieving metabolic flexibility has many advantages for overall health and wellness, such as better control of blood sugar and weight management, reduced inflammation, and enhanced cognitive function.

IMPACT ON METABOLIC DISORDERS

Impaired metabolic flexibility is a hallmark of metabolic disorders such as metabolic syndrome, type 2 diabetes, and obesity. Understanding the effect of metabolic flexibility on these circumstances is significant for creating viable mediations. The following are some important insights into the connection between metabolic disorders and metabolic flexibility:

Obesity

Obesity is frequently accompanied by diminished metabolic flexibility. Reduced fat oxidation and an increased reliance on glucose as a fuel causes obesity-related impairments in the ability to switch between fuel sources. Insulin resistance and body fat accumulation are both exacerbated by metabolic inflexibility. Obesity-related metabolic abnormalities can be reduced and overall metabolic health improved by increasing metabolic flexibility through diet, exercise, and weight loss.

Type 2 Diabetes

The onset and progression of type 2 diabetes are significantly influenced by inflexibility in the metabolic system. People with type 2 diabetes frequently display an inability to switch between glucose and fat oxidation, prompting raised blood glucose levels and insulin obstruction. Insulin sensitivity can be improved, blood glucose control can be improved, and the risk of complications associated with diabetes can be reduced by enhancing metabolic flexibility, specifically by promoting the ability to effectively utilize fats as a fuel source.

Kidney Syndrome

A group of metabolic abnormalities known as metabolic syndrome includes central obesity, hypertension, dyslipidemia, and insulin resistance. Metabolic firmness is a typical element of metabolic disorder. Metabolism flexibility can help people with metabolic syndrome switch between fuel sources, increase fat utilization, and increase insulin sensitivity, all of which are important aspects of the syndrome.

Heart Health

Cardiovascular diseases like atherosclerosis and heart disease are closely linked to metabolic disorders. Dyslipidemia, elevated triglycerides, and low levels of high-density lipoprotein (HDL) cholesterol are all risk factors for cardiovascular disease that are exacerbated by impaired metabolic flexibility. Lipid profiles can be normalized, vascular function can be improved, and the risk of cardiovascular complications can be reduced by increasing metabolic flexibility.

Therapeutic Interventions

The management of metabolic disorders has shown promise for strategies aimed at increasing metabolic flexibility. It has been demonstrated that weight management, a balanced diet, regular physical activity, and lifestyle interventions can increase metabolic flexibility and health. In addition, specific nutritional interventions, such as low-carbohydrate diets or intermittent fasting, may aid in the management of metabolic disorders and improve metabolic flexibility.

In both the prevention and treatment of metabolic disorders, one of the most important goals is to comprehend and enhance metabolic flexibility. Improve insulin sensitivity, optimize blood glucose control, encourage fat utilization, and reduce the risk of metabolic complications associated with obesity, type 2 diabetes, metabolic syndrome, and cardiovascular diseases by enhancing the body's ability to adaptively switch between fuel sources.

FACTORS INFLUENCING METABOLIC FLEXIBILITY

Numerous factors, including genetic and lifestyle-related factors, influence metabolic flexibility. Some important factors that can affect metabolic flexibility are as follows:

Genetics

Hereditary variables assume a part in deciding a person's metabolic flexibility. The ability to switch between fuel sources can be affected by certain gene variations, which can affect metabolic pathways like those that are involved in insulin signaling, lipid metabolism, and mitochondrial function. Hereditary variables can likewise include to varieties in resting metabolic rate and supplement digestion.

Body Structure

Metabolic flexibility can be affected by body composition, particularly the ratio of lean mass to fat mass. Since muscle tissue is a major site for the utilization of glucose and fatty acids, higher levels of lean muscle mass have been linked to increased metabolic flexibility. Then again, expanded adiposity, particularly instinctive fat, is connected to disabled metabolic flexibility and insulin obstruction.

Active work

Metabolic flexibility can be significantly impacted by regular exercise and physical activity. Training for exercise makes it easier for muscles to use both glucose and fatty acids as fuel, which makes metabolism more flexible. It has been demonstrated that aerobic exercise and resistance training enhance metabolic flexibility by increasing mitochondrial function and insulin sensitivity.

Composition of Diet

Metabolic flexibility can be affected by a person's diet, particularly the ratio of macronutrients. Reduced metabolic flexibility, elevated insulin resistance, and impaired fat oxidation have been linked to diets high in refined carbohydrates and saturated fats. Then again, counts calories wealthy in whole food varieties, including vegetables, natural products, lean proteins, and solid fats, advance metabolic flexibility, and insulin sensitivity.

Calories Taken in

Metabolic flexibility can be affected by how much energy is used versus how many calories are consumed. In addition to contributing to insulin resistance, chronic overeating and consuming an excessive amount of calories can impair metabolic flexibility. On the other hand, insulin sensitivity and metabolic flexibility can be enhanced by calorie restriction and controlled energy intake.

Stress and sleep

Rest span and quality, also as feelings of anxiety, can impact metabolic flexibility. Disrupted metabolic function, insulin resistance, and impaired glucose tolerance have been linked to insufficient sleep and chronic stress. Supporting metabolic flexibility can be aided by placing a high value on getting enough sleep and employing strategies for stress management.

Hormonal Changes and Aging

As we get older, metabolic flexibility tends to decrease. Changes in hormones, like lower levels of testosterone and growth hormone, can affect metabolic flexibility and muscle mass. As people get older, it's becoming increasingly important to use methods like regular exercise and maintaining a healthy body composition to keep metabolic flexibility.

It is essential to keep in mind that there are individual variations and that these factors interact in a complex way. Modifications to one's lifestyle, such as exercising frequently, eating a well-balanced diet, getting sufficient sleep, and managing stress, have the potential to improve metabolic flexibility and support overall metabolic health.

WHAT ARE THE 6 WEEKS OF METABOLIC FLEXIBILITY

The 6 Weeks of Metabolic Flexibility aims to increase your body's capacity to switch between burning carbohydrates and fats for fuel based on what is available. This is referred to as metabolic flexibility, and it is an essential component of overall fitness and health. The program is separated into six stages, each with its purpose:

Fundamental

You will concentrate on strengthening your fundamental movement foundation and enhancing your cardiovascular fitness during this phase.

Adaptation

This phase is meant to make it easier for your body to get used to burning fat as fuel. To encourage your body to burn more fat, you will perform workouts with a focus on moderate to low-intensity exercise.

Conversion

To encourage your body to burn more carbohydrates while exercising while still maintaining your ability to burn fat, you will increase the intensity of your workouts during this phase.

Rhythm

You'll focus on creating a consistent exercise routine during this phase to help you long-term improve your metabolic flexibility.

Stride

This phase focuses on pushing yourself to new fitness levels by intensifying your workouts even more.

Downhill

Your workouts will be tapered down in the final phase to allow your body to recover and get ready for the next cycle of the program.

You will also learn around how to fuel your body for optimal performance throughout the program. The program is intended to be testing yet versatile to your wellness level.

WEEK 1: FUNDAMENTAL

Week 1 of Metabolic Flexibility focuses on fundamental principles of metabolic flexibility and incorporates healthy, whole food-based meals to support metabolic flexibility.

The key concepts that support the body's ability to efficiently switch between various energy sources in response to changing conditions are referred to as the principles of metabolic flexibility. The following are some of the fundamental tenets of metabolic flexibility:

Balanced Macronutrient Intake
Maintaining metabolic flexibility necessitates consuming a variety of macronutrients, including proteins, carbohydrates, and fats, in a well-balanced diet. For energy production and other physiological processes, the body requires all three macronutrients.

Timing of nutrients
For metabolic flexibility, it is also crucial to consume macronutrients at the right time. For instance, consuming carbohydrates at the right time can aid in enhancing insulin sensitivity and glucose tolerance, two essential aspects of metabolic flexibility.

Physical Activity
Standard active work is vital for Metabolic flexibility, as it improves the body's capacity to utilize different energy sources and advances insulin responsiveness.

Intermittent Fasting
Irregular fasting is a dietary procedure that includes rotating times of fasting and taking care of it. This approach can upgrade Metabolic flexibility by elevating the body's capacity to put away fat for energy.

Rest and Stress Management
Getting enough sleep and managing stress is important for keeping your metabolism flexible. Constant pressure and unfortunate rest quality can prompt dysregulation of chemicals and metabolic cycles, which can adversely affect Metabolic flexibility.

By following these standards, people can uphold their Metabolic flexibility and advance generally speaking well-being and health. It is vital to take note that singular requirements might fluctuate, and it is recommended to talk with a medical services supplier or enrolled dietitian for customized proposals.

Zucchini, and Pepper Jack Quiche

NUTRITION: Calories: 198kcal|Carbohydrates: 14g|Protein: 8g|Fat: 13g |Saturated Fat: 7g|Polyunsaturated Fat: 5g|Sodium: 289mg

INGREDIENTS:

- 1 pre-made pie crust (or make your own)
- 1 zucchini, chopped thin
- ½ cup diced green bell pepper
- Pepper Jack cheese, ½ cup, shredded
- freshly cracked black pepper, ¼ teaspoon
- eggs, 4
- heavy cream, ½ cup
- chopped onion, half cup
- chopped red bell pepper, half cup
- salt, ½ teaspoon
- olive oil, one tbsp.

INSTRUCTIONS:

a) Set the oven to 375°F.
b) In a sizeable griddle, warm the olive oil to a medium temperature.
c) Cook the zucchini, onion, red bell pepper, and green bell pepper till soft for around 10 mins.
d) Roll out the pie covering and fit it into a nine-inch pie plate.
e) Cover the bottom of the pie crust with half of the shredded Pepper Jack cheese.
f) Spread the sautéed vegetables on top of the cheese.
g) Inside a mixing container, mix the eggs, heavy cream, salt, and freshly cracked black pepper.
h) Sprinkle the vegetables with the egg mixture.
i) On top, drizzle with the rest of the Pepper Jack cheese.
j) Bake the quiche in a Preheated broiler for thirty-five to forty mins, till the filling is set and the top is brilliant brown.
k) Before slicing and serving, let the quiche cool slightly.

Chive and Gruyère Frittata with Crab and Bacon

NUTRITION: Calories:203| Fat: 17 g | Carbohydrates: 2 Fiber: 1 g | Protein: 13g|Sodium 278.3 mg

INGREDIENTS:

- 8 eggs
- heavy cream, ½ cup
- freshly cracked black pepper and salt
- bacon, cooked and crumbled, 4 slices
- cooked crab meat, ½ pound
- grated Gruyère cheese, ½ cup
- chopped chives, ¼ cup
- 1 avocado, diced
- olive oil, 1 tbsp

INSTRUCTIONS:

a) In a sizeable dish, combine the eggs, heavy cream, Gruyère cheese, chives, salt, and pepper.
b) Warm the olive oil and cook bacon and crab meat for around 3 mins.
c) Top the bacon and crab with the egg and cheese mixture and cook for 5 mins, till the edges are firm and set.
d) Set the oven to 350 °F and prepare for around 18 mins, till the center is set and the top is brown.
e) Take the pan out of the oven and let it cool for a couple of mins prior to serving.
f) Serve the frittata immediately with the avocado diced on top.

Keto Pancakes

NUTRITION: Calories: 192kcal|Carbohydrates: 6g|Protein: 9g|Fat: 16g |Sodium: 109mg|Potassium: 35mg|Fiber: 3g

INGREDIENTS:

- eggs, 4
- baking powder, 1 teaspoon
- unsweetened almond milk, ¼ cup
- coconut flour, ¼ cup
- Cinnamon, ¼ teaspoon (if desired)
- salt, ¼ teaspoon
- vanilla extract, 1 teaspoon (if desired)
- coconut oil, melted, 2 tbsps

INSTRUCTIONS:

a) In a sizeable dish, beat the eggs and almond milk thoroughly.
b) Separately whisk together the coconut flour, baking powder, salt, cinnamon, and vanilla extract (if utilizing) till smooth.
c) Set to the side for a couple of moments to permit the coconut flour to absorb the fluid.
d) Dissolve butter in a nonstick skillet or griddle across moderate flame.
e) Whisk in the dissolved coconut oil till well combined.
f) Using a ¼ cup measuring cup, pour the batter onto the skillet or griddle.
g) Cook for around 3 mins for each side, till brilliant brown and very much cooked.
h) Serve with sugar-free maple syrup, whipped cream, berries, or chopped nuts.

Banana Nut Muffins

NUTRITION: Calories 198|Fat 1g|Carbohydrates 47g|Protein 5g | Sodium18mg

INGREDIENTS:

- almond flour, 1½ cups
- ½ teaspoon baking soda
- Melted coconut oil, ¼ cup
- vanilla extract, 1 teaspoon
- ¼ cup honey or maple syrup
- ½ cup chopped walnuts
- salt, ¼ teaspoon
- baking powder, 1 teaspoon
- mashed ripe bananas, 3
- eggs, 2

INSTRUCTIONS:

a) Prepare a biscuit tin with paper liners and Set the broiler to 350°F.
b) Combine the salt, baking powder, baking soda, and almond flour in a dish.
c) In a substantial dish, combine the mashed bananas, eggs, honey or maple syrup, melted coconut oil, and vanilla extract.
d) Combine the dry and wet components till just combined.
e) Combine in the chopped walnuts.
f) Place roughly two-thirds of the batter in each muffin cup.
g) Bake for around twenty-five mins, till a toothpick introduced into the center comes out clean.
h) After around 8 mins in the pot, transfer the muffins to a wire stand to cool entirely.

Bacon Egg Cups

NUTRITION: Calories: 111.0;Saturated Fat: 2.7 g;Protein: 8.2 g;Total Fat: 8.1 g

INGREDIENTS:

- Bacon, 12 slices
- shredded cheddar cheese, ½ cup
- salt, ¼ teaspoon
- large eggs, 8
- freshly cracked black pepper, quarter tsp
- heavy cream, quarter cup
- 1 tbsp sliced fresh chives (if desired)

INSTRUCTIONS:

a) Lightly butter a 12-cup muffin pan and Preset the oven to 375°F.
b) Slice every bacon piece in half and arrange two halves in a crisscross pattern in every muffin cup.
c) In a dish, whisk the eggs, heavy cream, salt, and freshly cracked black pepper till well combined.
d) Incorporate the shredded cheddar cheese and (if using) the chives.
e) Pour roughly a third of the egg mixture into every muffin cup.
f) Bake the bacon egg cups in a preheated oven for around 25 mins, till the eggs are set.
g) Before loosening the edges and removing the cups from the tin, allow them to cool for a few mins.

Breakfast Burrito Bowl

NUTRITION: Calories: 130| Fat: 11.1g | Carbohydrates: 6.1g | Fiber: 2.3g | Sugars: 2.9g | Protein: 3.3g | Sodium: 45mg

INGREDIENTS:

- ½ pound ground breakfast sausage
- eggs, 4
- diced red bell pepper, quarter cup
- freshly cracked black pepper and salt
- diced green bell pepper, quarter cup
- ½ avocado, sliced
- shredded cheddar cheese, quarter cup
- diced onion, quarter cup
- Salsa, quarter cup

TOPPINGS

- sliced cilantro, diced tomato, sliced jalapeño, sour cream

INSTRUCTIONS:

a) Cook the ground morning sausage in a sizeable skillet across moderate-high flame.
b) Cook the bacon for 6 mins, till it is crispy and browned.
c) Separate the sausage from the skillet and layer it on top of the diced bell peppers and onion. Cook for around 4 mins, stirring frequently.
d) Whisk the eggs with the salt and pepper. Put aside.
e) Pour in the whisked eggs.
f) Scramble the eggs for around 3 mins, till completely cooked.
g) Separate the sausage, veggies, and scrambled eggs into two separate bowls.
h) Include shredded cheddar cheese, sliced avocado, and salsa to every bowl.
i) Toppings such as sliced cilantro, diced tomato, sliced jalapeño, or a dollop of sour cream can be added if desired.

Masala Chicken with Brown Butter Spinach

NUTRITION: Calories 356 | 25g Fats | 9g Carbohydrates | 25g Protein | Sodium 174 mg

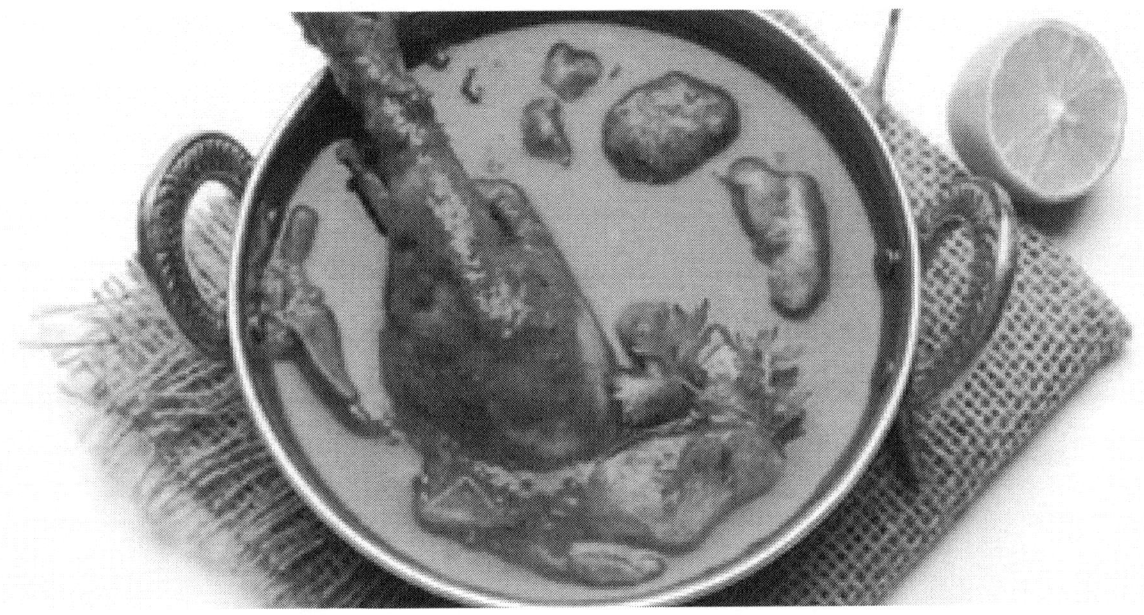

INGREDIENTS:

FOR THE CHICKEN:

- olive oil, two tbsps
- ground turmeric, ½ tsp
- freshly cracked black pepper and salt
- bone-in, skin-on chicken thighs, 6 pieces
- garam masala, 2 tbsps
- garlic powder, ½ tsp

FOR THE SPINACH:

- baby spinach, 6 cups
- freshly cracked black pepper and salt
- unsalted butter, 2 tbsps
- minced garlic, 3 cloves

INSTRUCTIONS:

a) Set the oven to 400°F.
b) Combine garam masala, garlic powder, turmeric, salt, and pepper in a dish.
c) Rub the olive oil all over the chicken thighs before coating them with the spice mixture.
d) Bake for around 30 mins in a warmed up oven, till golden brown and cooked through.
e) Prepare the spinach with garlicky brown butter while the chicken is cooking.
f) In a sizeable skillet, melt the butter across moderate flame till it starts to foam.
g) In a skillet, cook the garlic for 2 mins till fragrant.
h) Cook the baby spinach in a skillet till it is shriveled, around 4 mins. To taste, drizzle with salt and pepper.
i) Put a tbsp of the garlicky brown butter spinach on top of the chicken thighs.

Pork Chops with Romesco Butter and Broccoli

NUTRITION: Calories 421| 43g Fats| 5g Carbohydrates| 27g Protein |Sodium 98 mg

INGREDIENTS:

FOR THE PORK CHOPS:
- olive oil, one tbsp
- garlic powder, ½ tsp
- freshly cracked black pepper and salt
- smoked paprika, 1 tsp
- bone-in pork chops, 2

FOR THE ROMESCO BUTTER:
- unsalted butter, 2 tbsps
- lemon juice, one tsp
- freshly cracked black pepper and salt
- Romesco sauce, 1 tbsp

FOR THE BROCCOLI:
- freshly cracked black pepper and salt
- olive oil, two tbsps
- garlic, crushed, two cloves
- broccoli, slice into small florets, 1 head
- shredded Manchego cheese, quarter cup

INSTRUCTIONS:

a) Set the oven to 400°F.
b) Rub pork chops with salt, pepper, garlic powder, and smoked paprika.
c) In a sizeable skillet, heat the olive oil to a moderate-high temperature.
d) Cook the pork slashes for around 4 mins for every side, till sautéed and cooked through.
e) In a small dish, combine the butter, Romesco sauce, lemon juice, salt, and pepper for the romesco butter.
f) In a different container, throw the broccoli florets with the olive oil, garlic, salt, and pepper.
g) Roast the broccoli florets in a roasting pan for 12 mins till delicate and marginally caramelized.
h) After the pork chops have been removed from the skillet, put them away to rest for a few minutes.
i) Dissolve the romesco spread in a similar skillet across moderate flame.
j) Combine till completely combined.
k) Spoon the romesco butter over the pork chops and serve. Sprinkle with shredded Manchego cheese and top with roasted broccoli florets.

Stuffed Chicken Breasts with Balsamic Kale

NUTRITION: 244 Calories| 10g Fat (2g Saturated)| 47mg Cholesterol |314mg Sodium| 19g Carbohydrates (8g fiber| 11g Sugar | 0g Added)| 25g Protein

INGREDIENTS:

FOR THE CHICKEN:

- quarter cup sliced fresh parsley
- boneless, skinless chicken breasts, 4 pieces
- freshly cracked black pepper and salt
- goat cheese, 4 ounces
- ½ cup Kalamata olives, sliced

FOR THE KALE:

- Sliced kale, 1 bunch
- balsamic vinegar, 2 tbsps
- freshly cracked black pepper and salt
- unsalted butter, 2 tbsps

INSTRUCTIONS:

a) Set the oven to 375°F.
b) Combine the parsley, olives, and goat cheese in a small dish. To taste, sprinkle with salt and pepper.
c) Slice a pocket in the densest part of each chicken breast with care, making sure not to slice through the other side.
d) Fill every chicken breast pocket with the goat cheese and olive mixture and secure with toothpicks.
e) Dissolve the butter in an oven-safe skillet across moderate-high flame. Cook till the two sides of the stuffed chicken breasts are sautéed, around 4 mins for every side.
f) Bake the chicken for around 25 mins after it has been browned till it is cooked through and no longer pink in the center.

MAKE THE BALSAMIC-BUTTERED GREENS

g) In a sizeable skillet, dissolve the butter across moderate flame.
h) Cook the kale for around 6 mins till it is shriveled.
i) Toss the kale in the skillet with the balsamic vinegar to coat it. Include salt and pepper as required.
j) Prior to serving, rest the chicken for a few mins.
k) Serve the goat cheese and olive-stuffed chicken breasts with balsamic-buttered greens on the side.

Sausage, Spinach, and Cheese-Stuffed Portobello

NUTRITION: 320 Calories | 31g Fats | 8g Carbohydrates | 5g Protein | 670mg Sodium

INGREDIENTS:

- portobello mushrooms, stems removed, 4
- baby spinach, sliced, 2 cups
- ground Italian sausage, ½ pound
- freshly cracked black pepper and salt
- olive oil, 2 tbsps
- diced onion, ½ cup
- grated Parmesan cheese, quarter cup
- Minced garlic, 2 cloves
- shredded mozzarella cheese, quarter cup

INSTRUCTIONS:

a) Set your oven to 375°F.
b) Break up the Italian sausage into tiny pieces and brown it in a sizeable skillet across moderate-high flame for around 6 mins, till browned and cooked all the way through.
c) Cook the sausage in the same skillet as the diced onion and minced garlic.
d) Continue to cook for another three mins.
e) Include the spinach to the skillet and stew for around three mins, till shriveled.
f) Stir in the shredded mozzarella and grated Parmesan cheese after removing the skillet from the heat. drizzle with salt and pepper.
g) Brush the portobello mushrooms with olive oil before placing them on a baking sheet.
h) Drizzle with salt and pepper to taste.
i) Spoon the sausage and spinach blend into every portobello mushroom cap, filling them to the top.
j) Prepare the stuffed mushrooms in the warmed-up oven for around 25 mins, till the mushrooms are delicate and the cheddar is liquefied and effervescent.

Poke Bowl

NUTRITION: Calories 330 |Fat 17.7g| Saturated fat 2.6g |Polyunsaturated fat 5.6|Cholesterol 109.1mg |Sodium 126.5mg|Carbohydrates 1g|Sugar 0g| Fiber 0.4g |Protein 39.5g

INGREDIENTS:

- Cubed sushi-grade salmon or tuna, 1 pound
- Minced garlic, 2 cloves
- grated ginger, 1 tsp
- sesame seeds, one tbsp
- soy sauce, quarter cup
- sesame oil, one tbsp
- sliced cucumber, 1 cup
- rice vinegar, one tbsp
- Honey, one tsp
- cooked white or brown rice, 3 cups
- sliced avocado, one cup
- chopped mango, one cup
- sliced scallions, quarter cup
- Sriracha or other hot sauce, for serving

INSTRUCTIONS:

a) Mix the soy sauce, sesame oil, rice vinegar, honey, garlic, and ginger inside a mixing container.
b) Coat the cubed salmon or tuna in the marinade in a mixing dish.
c) Refrigerate the bowl for at least 30 mins, but no more than an hour.
d) Prepare the rice according to package directions while the fish marinates.
e) Serve the prepared rice in four bowls.
f) Serve the marinated fish, cucumber slices, avocado slices, diced mango, and sliced scallions on top of every bowl of rice.
g) Top with sesame seeds.
h) On the side, serve the poke bowls with Sriracha or other hot sauce.

Low-Carb Burger Bowl

NUTRITION: 268 Calories| 21g Fats| 2g Carbohydrates| 15g Protein |Sodium 174 mg

INGREDIENTS:

- ground beef, 1 pound
- Salt and pepper, 1 pinch every
- Mayonnaise, 4 tbsps
- Ketchup, 2 tbsps
- tomatoes, diced, 2
- sliced red onion, 1
- cheddar cheese, 4 slices
- Mustard, 2 tbsps
- sliced lettuce, 4 cups
- olive oil, 2 tbsps
- Pickles, sliced (if desired)

INSTRUCTIONS:

a) Include salt and pepper to the ground beef.
b) Slice the ground beef mixture into four equal pieces and shape it into burger patties.
c) In a sizeable skillet, warm the olive oil to a moderate-high temperature.
d) Fry the hamburger patties in a skillet for around 4 mins on every side, till they are cooked through and lightly browned.
e) While the burgers are cooking, set up the extra fixings. In a sizeable dish, toss the slashed lettuce, diced tomatoes, and meagerly hacked red onion.
f) In a little dish, combine the mayonnaise, ketchup, and mustard to make the burger sauce.
g) When the burgers are finished, include a slice of cheddar on top of every one and let it soften for 2 mins.
h) Divide the lettuce mixture evenly among four bowls to make the burger bowls.
i) Drizzle the burger sauce over every bowl and top with a cooked burger patty.
j) Serve immediately with sliced pickles, if preferred.

Coconut Chicken

NUTRITION: Calories 356 | 25g Fats | 9g Carbohydrates | 25g Protein | Sodium 174 mg

INGREDIENTS:

- boneless, skinless chicken breasts, slice into strips, 4 parts
- onion powder, ½ tsp
- paprika, ½ tsp
- all-purpose flour, half cup
- garlic powder, half tsp
- salt, half tsp
- large eggs, 2
- unsweetened shredded coconut, half cup
- panko bread crumbs, half cup
- freshly cracked black pepper, quarter tsp
- Cooking oil, for frying

INSTRUCTIONS:

a) Set the oven to 375°F.
b) Inside a dish, mix the flour, salt, freshly cracked black pepper, onion powder, paprika, and garlic powder.
c) Separately beat the eggs in a shallow container.
d) Mix the panko bread crumbs and shredded coconut in a third dish.
e) Dredge every chicken strip in the mixture of flour, beaten eggs, coconut, and panko.
f) Warm the frying oil in a sizeable skillet across moderate-high flame.
g) Cook the coated chicken strips for four mins on every side, till they are crispy and golden brown.
h) Place the chicken tenders on a baking sheet and heat for a further 13 mins, till the chicken is cooked through and at this point not pink in the center.
i) Eliminate the chicken from the oven and lay it to the side for a couple of moments to cool before serving.
j) For a delightful and healthy lunch, serve the coconut chicken strips with your favorite dipping sauce or on top of a bed of greens.

Salmon Avocado Power Bowl

NUTRITION: Calories 330 |Fat 17.7g| Saturated fat 2.6g|Polyunsaturated fat 5.6|Cholesterol 109.1mg|Sodium 126.5mg |Carbohydrates 1g|Sugar 0g| Fiber 0.4g|Protein 39.5g

INGREDIENTS:

- fresh salmon fillet, 1 pound
- freshly cracked black pepper and salt
- cooked brown rice, one cup
- shredded kale or spinach, one cup
- olive oil, one tbsp
- cherry tomatoes, halved, half cup
- sliced red onion, quarter cup
- sliced fresh cilantro, quarter cup
- avocado, diced, one
- lime, slice into wedges, 1
- balsamic vinegar, 1 tbsp

INSTRUCTIONS:

a) Set the oven to 400°F.
b) On a parchment-lined baking sheet, season the salmon fillet with salt and pepper to taste.
c) In a preheated oven, prepare the salmon for 12-15 mins, till it's cooked through and flakes effectively with a fork.
d) While the salmon bakes, prepare the remaining components.
e) In a sizeable dish, combine the cooked brown rice, shredded spinach or kale, cherry tomatoes, red onion, and cilantro.
f) Whisk the olive oil and balsamic vinegar together to make a basic vinaigrette.
g) After adding the diced avocado to the sizeable blending container with the other components, sprinkle the vinaigrette across everything. Whisk everything together to combine.
h) When the salmon is finished, eliminate it from the oven and put it to the side to cool for a couple of moments.
i) Divide the rice and veggie mixture evenly between two bowls to make the power bowls.
j) Top with cooked fish and lime wedges.

Meatball Bowl

NUTRITION: 290 calories | 9g Fat | 3.5g saturated fat | 38g Carbohydrates | 7g dietary fiber | 13g protein | 25mg Sodium

INGREDIENTS:

- ground beef or turkey, one pound
- garlic powder, half tsp
- onion powder, one tsp
- almond flour, half cup
- fresh parsley, quarter cup sliced
- Egg, 1
- freshly cracked black pepper and salt
- cooked quinoa or brown rice, 2 cups
- steamed broccoli florets, 2 cups
- cherry tomatoes, one cup, sliced
- red onion, quarter cup, sliced
- olive oil, 1 tbsp.
- crumbled feta cheese, quarter cup
- sliced fresh cilantro, quarter cup
- one lemon, slice into wedges

INSTRUCTIONS:

a) Preset the oven to 400 degrees F.
b) Combine the ground turkey or beef, almond flour, sliced parsley, egg, garlic powder, onion powder, and salt and pepper as required in a sizeable dish. Mix everything to a smooth consistency.
c) Using your hands, shape the meat blend into 12-15 meatballs.
d) On a baking sheet coated with parchment paper, bake the meatballs for around 18 mins, till cooked through and gently browned.
e) Prepare the remaining components while the meatballs are baking.
f) In a sizeable dish, mix the cooked quinoa or brown rice, steamed broccoli florets, sliced cherry tomatoes, diced red onion, crumbled feta cheese, and sliced cilantro.
g) Drizzle the olive oil over the vegetable and grain mixture, then toss to incorporate.
h) Eliminate the meatballs from the oven and set them aside for a couple of mins to cool.
i) To make the meatball bowls, divide the vegetable and grain mixture evenly between the two bowls.
j) Top every serving with cooked meatballs and lemon wedges.

Chicken Burrito Bowl

NUTRITION: Calories 356 | 25g Fats | 9g Carbohydrates | 25g Protein | Sodium 174 mg

INGREDIENTS:

- Extra-virgin olive oil, one tbsp.
- chili powder, one tsp
- Diced tomatoes, 2
- Diced avocado, 1
- Sliced red onion, 1
- cooked brown rice or cauliflower rice, 1 cup
- cumin, one tsp
- paprika, half tsp
- garlic powder, quarter tsp
- sliced lettuce, four cups
- chicken breast, cubed, 1 pound
- freshly cracked black pepper and salt
- black beans, drained & washed, one cup
- lime, one, slice into wedges
- Cilantro, sliced (if desired)

INSTRUCTIONS:

a) In a little bowl, consolidate the chili powder, cumin, paprika, garlic powder, and salt and pepper.
b) In a sizeable skillet, heat the olive oil to a moderate-high temperature.
c) Cover the chicken in the skillet with the spice mixture.
d) Cook the chicken for 6 mins, till it is delicately cooked.
e) Mix the diced tomatoes, red onion, and sliced lettuce in a sizeable dish.
f) When the chicken is done, combine in the cooked brown rice or cauliflower rice.
g) Divide the lettuce mixture evenly among four bowls to make the burrito bowls.
h) Include the seasoned chicken and rice mixture, black beans, cubed avocado, and fresh lime juice to every bowl.
i) Garnish with cilantro, if desired.

Philly Cheese Steak Bowl

NUTRITION: Calories 390|Total Fat 17g |Saturated Fat 6g |Cholesterol 50mg |Sodium 930mg |Total Carbohydrate 42g |Dietary Fiber 1g |Sugars 4g

INGREDIENTS:

- flank steak, slice into strips, 1 pound
- bell peppers, sliced, 2
- onion, sliced, 1
- onion powder, one tsp
- freshly cracked black pepper and salt
- soy sauce, one tbsp
- garlic powder, half tsp
- olive oil, three tbsps
- Worcestershire sauce, two tbsps
- cooked rice or cauliflower rice, 4 cups
- shredded provolone cheese, 1 cup

INSTRUCTIONS:

a) Melt the butter in a sizeable skillet across moderate-high flame.
b) Incorporate one tbsp of olive oil.
c) Cook the slice flank steak for around 6 mins till it is browned. Put it away.
d) Include the remaining olive oil, sliced bell peppers, and sliced onion to the same skillet.
e) Cook the vegetables for around 6 mins till they are tender.
f) Toss the cooked steak in the skillet to combine.
g) In the skillet, include the Worcestershire sauce, soy sauce, garlic and onion powder, salt, and pepper. Include the sauce and stir to coat the meat and vegetables.
h) Distribute the cooked rice or cauliflower rice evenly among four bowls.
i) Serve the steak and veggie mixture on top of the rice.
j) Top with shredded provolone cheese.

Shrimp, and fennel stew

NUTRITION: Calories 54|Fat 0.5g grams|Saturated Fat 0.1g grams |Carbohydrates 0.5g grams|Fiber 0.1g grams |Sugars 0.1g grams|Protein 1.3g| Sodium 65mg

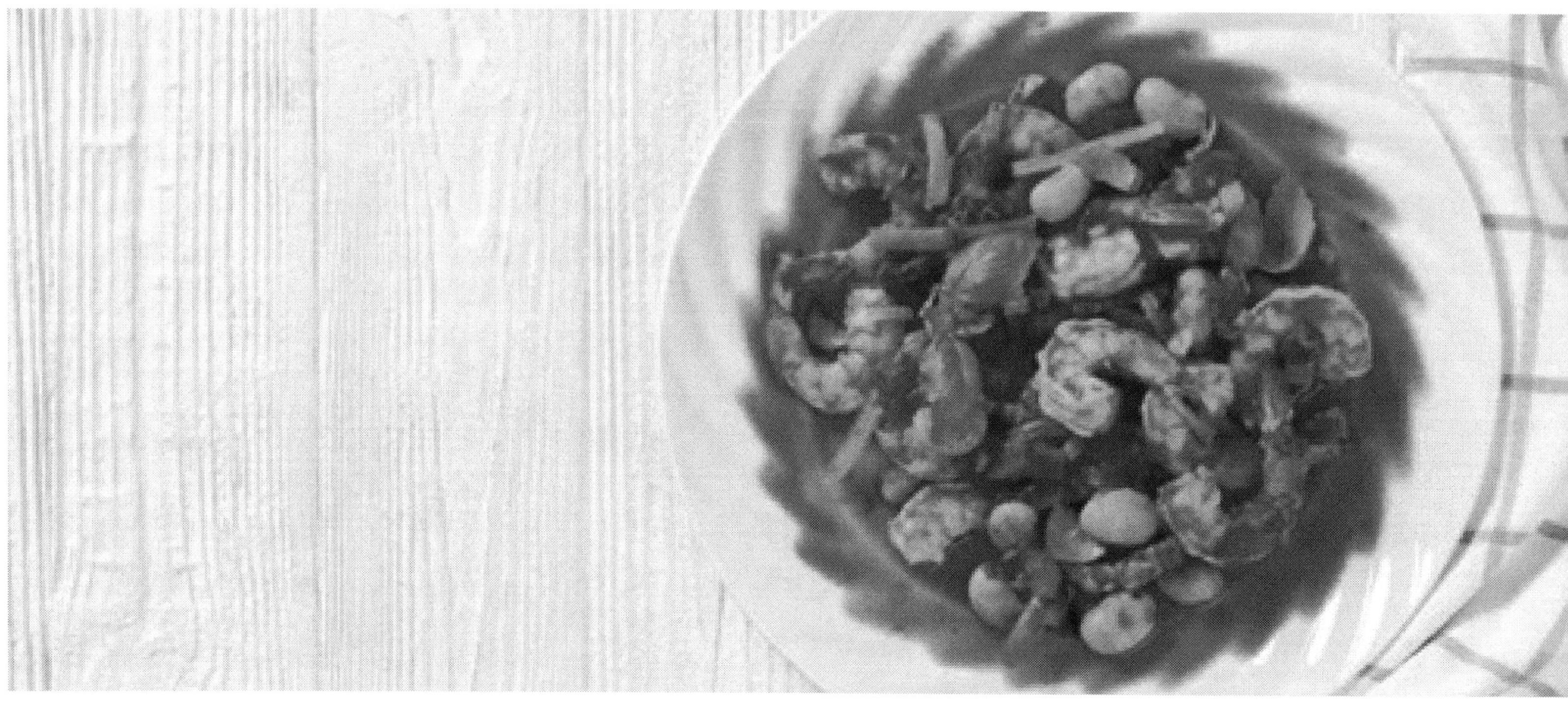

INGREDIENTS:

- shrimp, peeled and deveined,1 pound
- minced garlic, 3 cloves
- paprika, half tsp
- freshly cracked black pepper and salt
- olive oil, quarter cup
- Diced onion, 1
- chicken or vegetable broth, one cup
- diced tomatoes, one can
- fennel, thinly sliced, 2 bulbs
- dry white wine, quarter cup
- Fresh parsley, sliced for garnish

INSTRUCTIONS:

a) In a sizeable pot or Dutch broiler, warm the olive oil across moderate intensity.
b) Sauté the diced onion and sliced fennel for around 6 mins, till they are translucent and tender.
c) Cook for a further minute after adding the paprika and minced garlic.
d) Include white wine and bring the white wine to a simmer for three mins.
e) In a pot, bring the diced tomatoes and chicken or vegetable broth to a simmer.
f) Sprinkle salt and pepper over the shrimp in the pot.
g) Simmer the stew for around six mins, till the shrimp are pink and fully cooked.
h) Serve the stew immediately with parsley on top.

Mushrooms and Fresh Tomato Salad

NUTRITION: Calories: 374| Fat: 15.8g | Carbohydrates: 30.8g | Fiber: 5.2g | Sugars: 16.8 g | Protein: 31g | Sodium: 113.2mg

INGREDIENTS:

- 8 ounces sliced mushrooms
- 2 tomatoes, sliced
- olive oil, 2 tbsps
- quarter cup sliced red onion
- sliced fresh parsley, quarter cup
- balsamic vinegar, 2 tbsps
- freshly cracked black pepper and salt

INSTRUCTIONS:

a) Mix the sliced tomatoes, red onion, parsley, and mushrooms in a sizeable dish.
b) Mix the olive oil, balsamic vinegar, salt, and pepper in a little dish.
c) Incorporate the mushroom and tomato combine with the dressing.
d) Keep in the cooler for somewhere around 30 mins before serving.
e) Serve the mushroom and tomato salad alongside grilled chicken or on top of a green salad.

Enchilada Bowl

NUTRITION: Calories: 445| Fat: 29.6g | Carbohydrates: 9.5g | Fiber: 2.7g | Sodium: 189mg | Sugars: 2.9g | Protein: 33.2g

INGREDIENTS:

- ground beef or turkey, 1 pound
- 1 can (4 ounces) of diced green chilies
- freshly cracked black pepper and salt
- cooked rice, 1 cup
- ragged cheddar cheese, one cup
- black beans, drained and washed, 15-oz. can
- chopped tomatoes drained, 14-oz. can
- olive oil, one tbsp
- Sliced onion, one
- Crushed garlic, two cloves
- chili powder, one tbsp
- cumin, one tsp
- paprika, half tsp
- Fresh cilantro and lime wedges for garnish

INSTRUCTIONS:

a) Inside a pot, warm the olive oil and sauté the sliced onion.
b) Cook till the ground beef or turkey is browned in the skillet.
c) In the skillet, include and cook the minced garlic, chili powder, cumin, and paprika.
d) Stir together the black beans, diced tomatoes, and diced green chilies in the skillet. drizzle with salt and pepper.
e) Simmer on low for 15 mins.
f) Separately, combine the cooked rice and cheddar cheese.
g) Serve a scoop of the rice and cheese mixture followed by a dollop of the meat and bean combination.
h) Serve with fresh cilantro and a wedge of lime as garnish.

Roasted Miso Salmon with Green Beans

NUTRITION: Calories 330 |Fat 17.7g| Saturated fat 2.6g|Polyunsaturated fat 5.6|Cholesterol 109.1mg|Sodium 126.5mg |Carbohydrates 1g|Sugar 0g| Fiber 0.4g|Protein 39.5g

INGREDIENTS:

- salmon,4 fillets
- grated ginger, 1 tbsp
- miso paste, 2 tbsps
- Trimmed green beans, 1 pound
- sesame oil, one tbsp
- honey, two tbsps
- soy sauce, two tbsps
- orange juice, half cup
- freshly cracked black pepper and salt
- Sesame seeds and sliced green onions for garnish

INSTRUCTIONS:

a) Preset the oven to 400 degrees F.
b) Combine the honey, soy sauce, orange juice, miso paste, sliced ginger, and sesame oil in a small dish.
c) In a baking dish, pour the citrus-miso marinade over the salmon fillets.
d) Allow the salmon to marinate for around 18 mins.
e) Prepare the green beans while the fish is marinating.
f) Toss with salt, pepper, and olive oil in a mixing bowl.
g) In the baking dish, arrange the green beans around the fish.
h) Bake for 12-15 mins, till the salmon is cooked through and the green beans are soft and lightly browned.
i) Garnish the salmon and green beans with sesame seeds and sliced green onions.

Parmesan Zucchini Noodles with Shrimp

NUTRITION: Calories 12|Fat 0.3g grams|Saturated Fat 0.1g grams |Carbohydrates 0.5g grams|Fiber 0.1g grams |Sugars 0.1g grams|Protein 1.3g| Sodium 75mg

INGREDIENTS:

- grated Parmesan cheese, quarter cup
- freshly cracked black pepper and salt
- shrimp, skinned and deveined, one pound
- 4 cloves garlic, crushed
- 4 zucchinis, spiralized
- quarter cup heavy cream
- butter, two tbsps
- Fresh parsley, sliced for garnish

INSTRUCTIONS:

a) In a sizeable skillet, warm the olive oil and butter.
b) Include garlic and cook for one to two mins, till the garlic is sweet-smelling.
c) Inside a skillet, cook the shrimp for around 3 mins on every side, till they are pink and cooked through. Place aside.
d) In the same skillet, include the red pepper flakes, salt, and freshly cracked black pepper.
e) Cook, mixing intermittently, for around three mins, till the zucchini is delicately soft.
f) Include the Parmesan cheese and stir.
g) Return the cooked shrimp to the skillet and stir everything together.
h) Serve immediately, garnished with sliced parsley.

Roasted Cauliflower Steaks with Zucchini

NUTRITION: Calories: 130| Fat: 11.1g | Carbohydrates: 6.1g | Fiber: 2.3g | Sugars: 2.9g | Protein: 3.3g | Sodium: 45mg

INGREDIENTS:

- 1 head of cauliflower, sliced into 4-5 steaks
- 2 zucchinis, sliced
- 2 tsps garlic powder
- freshly cracked black pepper and salt
- olive oil, three tbsps
- smoked paprika, two tsps
- Fresh parsley, sliced for garnish

INSTRUCTIONS:

a) Preset the oven to 425 degrees F.
b) Prepare a baking pan with parchment paper.
c) Combine the salt, pepper, smoked paprika, garlic powder, and olive oil in a dish.
d) Use the mixture to brush the cauliflower steaks.
e) Put the cauliflower steaks on the baking sheet you prepared earlier. Cook for around 28 mins, till the vegetables are delicately soft.
f) Toss the zucchini slices with the rest of the olive oil mixture.
g) Include the zucchini slices to the oven sheet after fifteen mins and roast for additional 13 mins, till softer and lightly browned.
h) Allow the zucchini and cauliflower to cool for a couple of mins after the baking sheet has been removed from the oven.
i) On a platter, garnish the cauliflower steaks and zucchini slices with fresh parsley.

Steak Tip Cacciatore with Cauliflower Rice

NUTRITION: Calories 296| Total Fat 16g| Saturated Fat 5.9g | Trans Fat 0.6g| Polyunsaturated Fat 1g| Monounsaturated Fat 6.4g| Cholesterol 103mg; Sodium 639mg

INGREDIENTS:

- beef steak tips, trimmed and cubed, 1 pound
- sliced onion, one
- red bell pepper, sliced, one
- sliced mushrooms, one cup
- freshly cracked black pepper and salt
- olive oil, one tbsp
- chicken broth, half cup
- Minced garlic, two cloves
- green bell pepper, sliced, 1
- tomato paste, two tbsps
- dried basil, one tsp
- diced tomatoes, 14.5-ounce can
- dried oregano, 1 tsp
- Riced cauliflower, 1 head
- butter, 2 tbsps

INSTRUCTIONS:

a) Inside a sizeable skillet, warm the olive oil.
b) Include the steak and sear it for 5 mins, till all sides of the steak tips are browned. Place aside.
c) In the similar skillet, cook the onion and garlic for three mins till the onion is translucent.
d) Include the mushrooms and green and red bell peppers and cook for five mins.
e) In a dish, combine the tomato paste, basil, oregano, salt, and pepper with the sliced tomatoes. Cook for ten mins, till the sauce thickens, after bringing to a boil.
f) Melt the butter in a separate skillet across moderate flame. Include the cauliflower rice, and cook for around 6 mins, till the cauliflower is delicately tender.
g) Split the cauliflower rice between serving plates and top with the cacciatore steak tip.

Salisbury Steaks with Rosemary-Buttered

NUTRITION: Calories 296| Total Fat 16g| Saturated Fat 5.9g| Trans Fat 0.6g | Polyunsaturated Fat 1g| Monounsaturated Fat 6.4g | Cholesterol 103mg| Sodium 639mg

INGREDIENTS:

FOR THE SALISBURY STEAKS:
- 1 pound ground beef
- half cup breadcrumbs
- Milk, quarter cup
- 1 egg
- Worcestershire sauce, one tsp
- garlic powder, half tsp
- freshly cracked black pepper and salt
- 1 onion, sliced
- 2 cups beef broth
- olive oil, 1 tbsp
- 2 tbsps cornstarch

FOR THE ROSEMARY-BUTTERED POTATOES:
- potatoes, sliced into rounds, 4 moderate-sized
- unsalted butter softened, quarter cup
- sliced fresh rosemary, one tbsp
- freshly cracked black pepper and salt

INSTRUCTIONS:

a) Combine the breadcrumbs, milk, egg, Worcestershire sauce, garlic powder, salt, and pepper in a sizeable dish. To make oval-shaped patties, divide the components into four equal pieces.
b) In a sizeable skillet, warm the olive oil to a moderate-high temperature. Cook onion for around 6 mins, till the onion is translucent and somewhat sautéed. Set the onion aside after removing it from the skillet.
c) In the same skillet, brown and cook the meat patties for around 6 mins for every side, till sautéed and cooked through. Set the burgers aside after removing them from the griddle.
d) Combine the cornstarch and beef broth in a small dish. Heat the mixture to the point of boiling in a skillet. Cook for another four mins, till the sauce has thickened, at low heat.
e) Meanwhile, in a different skillet across moderate-high intensity, dissolve the butter. Dice the potatoes and combine them with the rosemary, salt, and pepper in a dish. Cook, stirring frequently, for ten-twelve mins, till the potatoes are browned and tender.
f) Place a beef patty on a plate and top with the onion and sauce to serve. Serve with rosemary-buttered potatoes.

FUNDAMENTAL SNACKS AND DESSERTS

Lurnea coconut Log

NUTRITION: Calories: 179| Fat: 16.8g | Carbs: 7.3g | Fiber: 2.4g| Sugars: 2.9g | Protein: 3.4g | Sodium: 120.5mg

INGREDIENTS:

- 1 can of sweetened condensed milk
- shredded coconut, 2 cups
- 250g plain sweet biscuits, crushed
- 2 tbsps cocoa powder
- Extra coconut for rolling

INSTRUCTIONS:

a) Combine the sweetened condensed milk, broken biscuits, shredded coconut, and cocoa powder.
b) Prepare a rectangle baking dish with parchment paper and equally distribute the mixture in it.
c) Refrigerate the mixture for at least 2 hours, till it is solid.
d) Eliminate the mixture from the fridge and slice it into logs with a sharp knife when it is solid.
e) Roll every log in more coconut till completely covered.
f) Chill the Lurnea coconut logs before serving.

Simple Egg Salad

NUTRITION: Calories:203| Fat: 17 g | Carbohydrates: 2 Fiber: 1 g | Protein: 13g|Sodium 278.3 mg

INGREDIENTS:

- sliced fresh parsley, one tbsp
- Dijon mustard, one tbsp
- hard-boiled eggs, skinned & sliced, six
- Mayonnaise, quarter cup
- freshly cracked black pepper and salt

INSTRUCTIONS:

a) In a dish, combine the sliced hard-boiled eggs, mayonnaise, Dijon mustard, and fresh parsley.
b) drizzle with salt & pepper as required.
c) Serve right away as a sandwich stuffing, salad greens, or cracker topping.

Ham, Cheese, and Egg Rolls

NUTRITION: 300 Calories | 28g Fats | 7g Carbohydrates | 26g Protein | 902mg Sodium

INGREDIENTS:

- 8 eggs
- diced onion, quarter cup
- Butter, one tbsp
- freshly cracked black pepper and salt
- diced bell pepper, quarter cup
- diced ham, half cup
- shredded cheddar cheese, half cup

INSTRUCTIONS:

a) Set the oven to 375°F.
b) Whisk the eggs, salt, and pepper in a dish.
c) Dissolve the butter in a saucepan across moderate flame.
d) After the vegetables have softened, include the cubed ham, onion, and bell pepper.
e) Place the ham and vegetables on top of the egg mixture.
f) Cook the eggs till they are set but slightly runny.
g) Eliminate the skillet from the heat and top the eggs with the shredded cheese.
h) Utilizing a spatula, gently fold the eggs over the cheese.
i) Scoop the egg mixture into egg roll wrappers and roll them up tightly.
j) Bake the egg rolls for 13 mins, till they are crispy and golden brown.

Bacon-Stuffed Avocados

NUTRITION: Calories 421| 43g Fats| 5g Carbohydrates| 27g Protein | Sodium 98 mg

INGREDIENTS:

- diced tomato, 2 tbsps
- bacon, cooked and crumbled, 4 slices
- freshly cracked black pepper and salt
- lime juice, one tbsp
- sliced fresh cilantro, two tbsps
- chopped red onion, 2 tbsps
- ripe avocados, halved and pitted, 2

INSTRUCTIONS:

a) Preset oven to 350°F/175°C.
b) Scoop off a little amount of flesh from the center of every avocado half to make a well for the filling.
c) Inside a little container, combine bacon, diced red onion, diced tomato, cilantro, lime squeeze, salt, and pepper.
d) Pour the bacon combination into the avocado wells.
e) Bake for 13 mins, till the filling is hot and the avocados are mellowed to some degree.
f) Serve immediately, if desired, topped with additional cilantro.

Avocado Egg Boat

NUTRITION: Calories 12|Fat 0.3g grams|Saturated Fat 0.1g grams |Carbohydrates 0.5g grams|Fiber 0.1g grams |Sugars 0.1g grams|Protein 1.3g| Sodium 75mg

INGREDIENTS:

- freshly cracked black pepper and salt
- 2 ripe avocados
- shredded cheddar cheese, quarter cup
- 4 eggs
- diced tomato, quarter cup
- diced onion, quarter cup
- Sliced fresh parsley or cilantro (if desired)

INSTRUCTIONS:

a) Preset the oven to 425 °F(218, Celsius).
b) Slice the avocados in half lengthwise and eliminate the pit.
c) Make a small well for the egg by delicately scooping out some of the flesh from every side with a spoon.
d) Put the avocado halves on a parchment-lined baking sheet.
e) Crack an egg into every avocado half, being careful not to break the yolk.
f) Over the eggs, scatter the diced tomato, onion, and shredded cheese.
g) Include salt and pepper as required.
h) Bake the eggs for twenty mins, till they are set to your preference.
i) If desired, top with fresh parsley or cilantro.

WEEK 2: ADAPTATION

Week 2 of Metabolic Flexibility focuses on adapting your diet and lifestyle to support metabolic flexibility. This week includes meals and snacks that incorporate a variety of macronutrients and support the body's ability to adapt to changing dietary needs.

The body's capacity to adapt to changing conditions and maintain homeostasis is referred to as adaptation, and it is one of the fundamental concepts of metabolic flexibility. When confronted with stressors, for example, changes in diet or exercise, the body starts a progression of versatile reactions to keep up with metabolic capability.

One of the key transformations that happen because of changes in diet is the upregulation of chemicals engaged with the digestion of explicit macronutrients. For instance, when starch admission is decreased, the body builds the development of chemicals associated with the breakdown of fats for energy creation.

Adaptation involves alterations in gene expression, hormone levels, and metabolic pathways in addition to changes in enzyme production. For instance, during times of fasting, the body produces more growth hormones and changes its energy metabolism to use fat stored in the body as fuel.

Practice is another stressor that can prompt variations in Metabolic flexibility. The powerhouses of cells that produce energy through the breakdown of macronutrients are boosted by regular exercise. In addition, exercise can increase glucose uptake and insulin sensitivity, resulting in improved metabolic flexibility.

Even though adaptation is an essential component of metabolic flexibility, excessive or chronic stress can cause maladaptation and adverse health outcomes. For instance, ongoing pressure or overtraining can prompt dysregulation of chemical creation and diminished Metabolic flexibility.

In general, supporting metabolic flexibility and promoting overall health and wellness requires an understanding of adaptation. By consolidating different stressors, for example, changes in diet and exercise, people can advance versatile reactions and keep up with Metabolic flexibility over the long haul.

ADAPTATION BREAKFASTS

Greek Yogurt Breakfast Parfait

NUTRITION: Calories 260 | Protein 4.4 grams |Fat 2.9 grams |Carbohydrates 40.5 grams |Sodium 77 mg

INGREDIENTS:

- Greek yogurt, 1 cup
- granola, quarter cup
- mixed berries (fresh or frozen), half cup
- honey or maple syrup, 1 tsp

INSTRUCTIONS:

a) In a small container or glass, layer the Greek yogurt, berries, and granola.
b) If desired, drizzle with honey or maple syrup.

Avocado Toast with Eggs

NUTRITION: 94 Calories|16.4g carbohydrate |8.5g fiber |15.5g protein |Sodium 41 mg

INGREDIENTS:

- whole-grain bread, 1 slice
- Mashed avocado, half
- Egg, 1
- freshly cracked black pepper and salt
- red pepper flakes, one pinch

INSTRUCTIONS:

a) Toast the bread till it is done to your liking.
b) Cook the egg to your liking (fried, scrambled, or poached) while the bread toasts.
c) Top the toast with the mashed avocado and the cooked egg.
d) drizzle with salt, pepper, and pepper flakes.

Berry Nut Butter Smoothie

NUTRITION: Calories: 250|Fat: 4g|Carbohydrates: 53g|Protein: 19g |Sodium 11 mg

INGREDIENTS:

- mixed berries (fresh or frozen), 1 cup
- almond butter, 1 tbsp
- vanilla protein powder, one scoop
- unsweetened almond milk, one cup
- honey or maple syrup, one tsp

INSTRUCTIONS:

a) Mix the entire components in a mixer & mix till uniform.
b) If the smoothie is excessively thick, include more almond milk till the ideal consistency is reached.

Blueberry Almond Protein Smoothie

NUTRITION: Calories: 46| Fat: 0.3g | Carbohydrates: 11g | Fiber: 2.8g | Sugars: 7.3g | Protein: 0.7g | Sodium: 2.8mg

INGREDIENTS:

- ripe banana, 1
- unsweetened almond milk, half cup
- blueberries, frozen, one cup
- vanilla protein powder, one scoop
- honey or maple syrup, 1 tsp

INSTRUCTIONS:

a) Blend all of the components till smooth.

Peanut Butter Banana Toast

NUTRITION: Calories: 130| Fat: 11.1g | Carbohydrates: 6.1g | Fiber: 2.3g | Sugars: 2.9g | Protein: 3.3g | Sodium: 45mg

INGREDIENTS:

- Sliced banana, half
- whole-grain bread, 1 slice
- natural peanut butter, 1 tbsp
- drizzle of cinnamon

INSTRUCTIONS:

a) Toast the bread till it is done to your liking.
b) Top the toast with the peanut butter and the sliced banana.
c) If desired, drizzle with cinnamon.

Green Smoothie Bowl

NUTRITION: Calories 70|Total Fat 0.5g| Carbohydrates 15g|Protein 1g | Sodium 39.2mg

INGREDIENTS:

- mixed greens, 1 cup
- frozen mango chunks, half cup
- unsweetened almond milk, half cup
- frozen banana, half

TOPPINGS

- sliced banana, chia seeds, granola, nuts

INSTRUCTIONS:

a) In a blender, combine the mixed greens, frozen banana, frozen mango, and almond milk and mix till uniform.
b) Fill a bowl halfway with the smoothie and top with sliced banana, chia seeds, granola, or nuts, if preferred.

Breakfast Tacos

NUTRITION: Calories 292.5|Total Fat 6.0 g|Saturated Fat 1.8 g |Sodium 1,198.7 mg|Potassium 634.2 mg |Total Carbohydrate 29.2 g|Dietary Fiber 7.2 g |Sugars 3.3 g|Protein 31.1 g

INGREDIENTS:

- Salsa and hot sauce to your taste
- 2 corn tortillas
- quarter cup black beans, drained and rinsed
- eggs, 2, scrambled
- quarter avocado, sliced
- shredded cheese, sliced cilantro

INSTRUCTIONS:

a) Cook the corn tortillas for 2 mins on every side in a dry skillet across low flame.
b) Divide the scrambled eggs, avocado slices, and black beans among the two tortillas.
c) As desired, top with salsa, hot sauce, shredded cheese, and sliced cilantro.

Bacon and Veggie Frittata

NUTRITION: Calories:203| Fat: 17 g | Carbohydrates: 2 Fiber: 1 g | Protein: 13g|Sodium 278.3 mg

INGREDIENTS:

- eggs, 4
- freshly cracked black pepper and salt
- shredded cheese
- diced cooked bacon, half cup
- half cup diced vegetables (bell peppers, onions, mushrooms, etc.)

INSTRUCTIONS:

a) Preset the oven to 375 Fahrenheit (190 Celsius).
b) Whisk the eggs, salt, and pepper inside a blending container.
c) In a cast-iron pan or oven-safe skillet, sauté the diced vegetables till tender.
d) In the skillet, stir in the cooked bacon to combine with the vegetables.
e) Cook the vegetables and bacon for around three mins on the stovetop after pouring the egg mixture over them.
f) Bake the skillet for twelve-fifteen mins, till the eggs are set, in the oven.
g) If desired, drizzle shredded cheese on top of the frittata and bake for a further 2 mins, till the cheese is dissolved.
h) Serve after cutting into slices.

Egg and Vegetable Muffins

NUTRITION: 77 Calories | 8g Fats | 0.7g Carbohydrates | 4.1g Protein | 438.9mg Sodium

INGREDIENTS:

- 6 eggs
- half cup diced vegetables (bell peppers, onions, spinach, etc.)
- freshly cracked black pepper and salt
- shredded cheese

INSTRUCTIONS:

a) Preset the oven to 350°F.
b) In a dish, mix the eggs, salt, and pepper.
c) Divide the diced vegetables among six muffin cups evenly.
d) Include the egg mixture to two-thirds of every muffin cup.
e) If desired, top the muffins with shredded cheese.
f) Bake the muffins for around 18 mins, till they are firm and lightly browned on top.
g) Prior to serving, allow the dish to cool for a few mins.

Chicken Caesar Salad

NUTRITION: Calories: 374| Fat: 15.8g | Carbohydrates: 30.8g | Fiber: 5.2g | Sugars: 16.8 g | Protein: 31g | Sodium: 113.2mg

INGREDIENTS:

- romaine lettuce, sliced, two cups
- grated Parmesan cheese, two tbsps
- Sliced grilled chicken breast, 4 ounces
- Croutons, quarter cup
- Caesar dressing, 2 tbsps

INSTRUCTIONS:

a) In a bowl, combine the sliced romaine lettuce.
b) Serve with grilled chicken breast slices, croutons, and grated Parmesan cheese on top.
c) Drizzle with dressing and toss.

Turkey and Hummus Wrap

NUTRITION: Calories 292.5|Total Fat 6.0 g|Saturated Fat 1.8 g |Sodium 1,198.7 mg|Potassium 634.2 mg|Total Carbohydrate 29.2 g|Dietary Fiber 7.2 g|Sugars 3.3 g|Protein 31.1 g

INGREDIENTS:

- 1 whole wheat tortilla
- quarter avocado, sliced
- quarter cup mixed greens
- 2 tbsps hummus
- 2 slices of turkey
- freshly cracked black pepper and salt

INSTRUCTIONS:

a) On the whole wheat tortilla, spread the hummus.
b) Top with turkey pieces, avocado, and mixed greens.
c) Top with salt and pepper.
d) Roll the wrap and slice it in half.

Grilled Chicken Avocado Salad

NUTRITION: Calories 356 | 25g Fats | 9g Carbohydrates | 25g Protein | Sodium 174 mg

INGREDIENTS:

- mixed greens, 2 cups
- grilled chicken breast, sliced, 4 ounces
- olive oil, one tbsp
- balsamic vinegar, one tbsp
- freshly cracked black pepper and salt
- avocado, sliced, half
- cherry tomatoes, shared, quarter cup
- cucumber, sliced, quarter cup
- red onion, sliced, quarter cup

INSTRUCTIONS:

a) In a bowl, combine the mixed greens.
b) Serve with grilled chicken breast slices, avocado, cherry tomatoes, cucumber, and red onion on top.
c) Sprinkle with olive oil and balsamic vinegar, and drizzle with salt & pepper.

Tuna Salad Lettuce Wraps

NUTRITION: Calories 326 | 45g Fats | 5g Carbohydrates | 39g Protein | 700mg Sodium

INGREDIENTS:

- quarter cup diced red onion
- Greek yogurt, quarter cup
- Lettuce leaves for wrapping
- Dijon mustard, 1 tbsp
- 2 cans tuna, drained
- quarter cup diced celery
- freshly cracked black pepper and salt

INSTRUCTIONS:

a) Begin by emptying the tuna can into a mixing dish.
b) Include the mayonnaise, Dijon mustard, sliced celery, sliced red onion, salt, and pepper.
c) Spoon a tiny quantity of tuna salad onto every lettuce leaf.
d) Tuck the sides of the lettuce leaf in as you roll it over the tuna salad.

Broccoli Cheddar Soup

NUTRITION: Calories 370|Fat 9g|Saturated fat 5g| Carbohydrate 57g |Dietary fiber 25g|Protein 20g | Sodium 90.67mg

INGREDIENTS:

- Butter, 1 tbsp
- heavy cream, half cup
- shredded cheddar cheese, half cup
- freshly cracked black pepper and salt
- Minced garlic, 1 clove
- sliced onion, half cup
- sliced broccoli florets, two cups
- chicken broth, two cups

INSTRUCTIONS:

a) Dissolve the butter in a sizeable pan across moderate flame.
b) Sauté the diced onion and minced garlic till soft.
c) Include the chicken broth to the pot along with the sliced broccoli florets.
d) Raise to a boil, afterwards cook the broccoli over low flame till tender.
e) Using a mixer, puree the soup till uniform.
f) Blend the grated cheddar cheese with the heavy cream till uniform.
g) Season as required with salt and pepper.

Quinoa and Vegetable Stir-Fry

NUTRITION: 250 Calories| 9g Fat (4g Saturated)| 17mg Cholesterol | 262mg Sodium| 33g Carbohydrates (5g fiber| 4g Sugar | 0g Added)| 9g Protein

INGREDIENTS:

- cooked quinoa, 1 cup
- bell pepper, sliced, half
- snow peas, half cup
- olive oil, one tbsp
- soy sauce, one tbsp
- freshly cracked black pepper and salt
- onion, sliced, half
- carrot, sliced, 1

INSTRUCTIONS:

a) In a skillet across moderate-high flame, warm the olive oil.
b) In the skillet, sauté the bell pepper, onion, carrot, and snow peas till tender.
c) Include the cooked quinoa and combine well.
d) Drizzle with soy sauce and season as required with salt and pepper.

Sweet Potato and Black Bean Bowl

NUTRITION: Calories 460|Fat 23g grams|Saturated Fat 9g grams |Sodium 1000mg milligrams|Carbohydrates 24g grams |Fiber 4g grams|Sugars 7g grams|Protein 40g grams

INGREDIENTS:

- chili powder, 1 tsp
- sweet potato, peeled and diced, 1
- olive oil, 1 tbsp
- black beans, drained & washed, one can
- green bell pepper, chopped, half
- red onion, diced, half
- red bell pepper, chopped, half
- cumin, half tsp
- freshly cracked black pepper and salt

INSTRUCTIONS:

a) Preset the oven to 400 degrees F.
b) Inside a blending container, mix the olive oil, chili powder, cumin, red and green bell peppers, red onion, and salt and pepper.
c) Roast the vegetables for around thirty mins, till they are soft, on a baking sheet.
d) Serve with roasted vegetables and black beans.

Mediterranean Tuna Bowl

NUTRITION: Calories 320 | 45g Fats | 5g Carbohydrates | 39g Protein | 700mg Sodium

INGREDIENTS:

- tuna, drained, 1 can
- sliced cucumber, quarter cup
- lemon juice, one tbsp
- freshly cracked black pepper and salt
- sliced tomatoes, quarter cup
- sliced red onion, quarter cup
- crumbled feta cheese, quarter cup
- olive oil, one tbsp

INSTRUCTIONS:

a) Combine the drained tuna, cucumber, tomatoes, red onion, and crumbled feta cheese in a mixing dish.
b) Include the juice of lemon, olive oil, salt, and pepper.

Turkey and Vegetable Soup

NUTRITION: Calories 292.5|Fat 6g|Saturated Fat 1.8 g|Sodium 1,198.7 mg |Potassium 634.2 mg|Total Carbohydrate 29.2 g|Protein 31.1 g

INGREDIENTS:

- olive oil, 1 tbsp
- chicken or turkey broth, 4 cups
- cooked turkey, shredded, 1 cup
- Minced garlic, 1 clove
- sliced onion, half cup
- sliced vegetables, 2 cups
- freshly cracked black pepper and salt

INSTRUCTIONS:

a) In a sizeable pot, warm the olive oil over low flame.
b) Sauté the minced garlic and sliced onion till soft.
c) In the pot, sauté the sliced vegetables till soft.
d) Bring the chicken or turkey stock to a bubble in the pot.
e) Simmer for around twenty-five mins, till the vegetables are delicately soft.
f) Include the cooked turkey till it is warmed completely in the pot.
g) Include pepper and salt and then serve.

Mexican-style Cauliflower Rice Bowl

NUTRITION: 132 Calories| 3g Fat (1g Saturated)| 90mg Cholesterol | 223mg Sodium| 14g Carbohydrates (3g fiber| 8g Sugar) | 15g Protein

INGREDIENTS:

- black beans, drained & washed, one can
- olive oil, one tbsp
- cauliflower rice, 2 cups
- yellow bell pepper, chopped, half
- green bell pepper, chopped, half
- red onion, chopped, half
- chili powder, one tsp
- cumin, half tsp
- freshly cracked black pepper and salt
- red bell pepper, diced, half
- Salsa and avocado for serving

INSTRUCTIONS:

a) Warm the olive oil in a saucepan across moderate-high flame.
b) Sauté the red onion and diced green, yellow, and red bell peppers till tender.
c) Include the black beans, salt, pepper, chili powder, and cumin to the cauliflower rice.
d) Cook the cauliflower rice for around 6 mins, till it is soft.
e) If desired, serve topped with salsa and avocado.

Grilled Chicken and Squash Kabobs

NUTRITION: Calories 356 | 25g Fats | 9g Carbohydrates | 25g Protein | Sodium 174 mg

INGREDIENTS:

- garlic powder, half tsp
- dried oregano, one tsp
- olive oil, one tbsp
- bell pepper, cubed, one
- zucchini, sliced, 1
- red onion, cubed, 1
- boneless, skinless chicken breasts, cubed, 2
- yellow squash, sliced, one
- freshly cracked black pepper and salt

INSTRUCTIONS:

a) Turn the grill up to moderate-high flame.
b) Thread the skewers with bell pepper, zucchini, yellow squash, chicken chunks, and red onion.
c) Brush olive oil on the skewers and drizzle with garlic powder, dried oregano, salt, and pepper.
d) Grill the skewers for ten mins, till the chicken is done and the veggies are soft.

Shrimp and Avocado Salad

NUTRITION: Calories 12|Fat 0.3g grams|Saturated Fat 0.1g grams |Carbohydrates 0.5g grams|Fiber 0.1g grams|Sugars 0.1g |Protein 1.3g| Sodium 75mg

INGREDIENTS:

- olive oil, two tbsps
- lime juice, two tbsps
- cooked shrimp, skinned and deveined, one lb.
- sliced cilantro, quarter cup
- avocados, diced, 2
- red onion, thinly sliced, quarter
- freshly cracked black pepper and salt

INSTRUCTIONS:

a) Combine the cooked shrimp, diced avocado, thinly sliced red onion, and cilantro in a sizeable mixing dish.
b) Finish with a sprinkle of olive oil, lime juice, and a drizzle of pepper and salt.

Broiled Salmon with Asparagus

NUTRITION: Calories: 130| Fat: 11.1g | Carbohydrates: 6.1g | Fiber: 2.3g | Sugars: 2.9g | Protein: 3.3g | Sodium: 45mg

INGREDIENTS:

- 2 salmon fillets
- olive oil, one tbsp
- freshly cracked black pepper and salt
- garlic powder, half tsp
- 1 bunch asparagus, trimmed

INSTRUCTIONS:

a) Set the oven to broil.
b) Place the salmon fillets and asparagus on a baking pan.
c) Finish by topping with a sprinkle of olive oil and a drizzle of garlic powder, salt, and pepper.
d) Broil for 10-12 mins, till the salmon is cooked through and the asparagus is soft.

Salmon Fillets with Roasted Veggies

NUTRITION: Calories: 259| Fat: 10.6g | Carbs: 7.3g | Fiber: 0.2g| Sugars: 2.4g | Protein: 33.4g | Sodium: 450mg

INGREDIENTS:

- 1 bell pepper, cubed
- 2 salmon fillets
- 1 yellow squash, sliced
- garlic powder, half tsp
- 1 red onion, cubed
- 1 zucchini, sliced
- olive oil, one tbsp
- freshly cracked black pepper and salt

INSTRUCTIONS:

a) Preset the oven to 400 degrees F.
b) On a baking sheet, organize the sliced vegetables and salmon fillets.
c) Season the top with salt, pepper, and garlic powder using olive oil.
d) Bake for about twenty-five mins, or till the vegetables are soft and the salmon is cooked through.

Zucchini Noodles with Shrimp and Pesto

NUTRITION: Calories 12|Fat 0.3g grams|Saturated Fat 0.1g grams |Carbohydrates 0.5g grams|Fiber 0.1g grams |Sugars 0.1g grams|Protein 1.3g| Sodium 75mg

INGREDIENTS:

- Pesto, half cup
- olive oil, 1 tbsp
- zucchini, spiralized, 2
- shrimp, skinned and deveined, one lb.
- freshly cracked black pepper and salt

INSTRUCTIONS:

a) Warm the olive oil in a saucepan across moderate-high flame.
b) Cook till the shrimp are pink and cooked through.
c) Cook till the spiralized zucchini is soft in the pan.
d) Cook till the pesto is cooked through, and then include the salt and pepper.

Cauliflower Crust Pizza

NUTRITION: 132 Calories| 3g Fat| 90mg Cholesterol| 223mg Sodium | 14g Carbohydrates (3g fiber| 8g Sugar)| 15g Protein

INGREDIENTS:

- cauliflower, riced, 1 head
- Egg, 1
- garlic powder, half tsp
- shredded mozzarella cheese, half cup
- dried oregano, half tsp
- almond flour, half cup
- tomato sauce, quarter cup

TOPPINGS

- sliced mushrooms, sliced bell pepper, and/or sliced onion

INSTRUCTIONS:

a) Set the oven to 425°F.
b) Combine the riced cauliflower, almond flour, egg, garlic powder, and dried oregano in a dish.
c) Using the cauliflower mixture, make a crust on a parchment-lined baking sheet.
d) Bake for around 20 mins, or till the crust turns golden brown.
e) Spread tomato sauce across the crust and top with shredded mozzarella cheese and any other desired toppings.
f) Continue baking for a further 13 mins, or till the cheese is bubbling and melted.

Lentil Veggie Soup

NUTRITION: Calories 370|Fat 9g|Saturated fat 5g| Carbohydrate 57g |Dietary fiber 25g|Protein 20g | Sodium 90.67mg

INGREDIENTS:

- dry brown lentils, rinsed and drained, 2 cups
- celery stalks, sliced, 2
- low-sodium chicken or vegetable broth, 6 cups
- Minced garlic, 2 cloves
- onion, sliced, one
- bay leaf, one
- dried thyme, one tsp
- carrots, peeled and sliced, 2
- freshly cracked black pepper and salt

INSTRUCTIONS:

a) Include the lentils, broth, onion, carrots, celery, garlic, thyme, and bay leaf to a pot.
b) Raise to a rolling boil and then gently simmer the mixture for around 35 mins, or till the lentils are soft.
c) Take out the bay leaf and season the soup with salt and pepper.

Beef and Broccoli with arrowroot powder

NUTRITION: Calories 296| Total Fat 16g| Saturated Fat 5.9g | Trans Fat 0.6g| Polyunsaturated Fat 1g| Monounsaturated Fat 6.4g| Cholesterol 103mg| Sodium 639mg

INGREDIENTS:

- flank steak, thinly sliced, 1 pound
- coconut aminos, quarter cup
- Minced garlic, 2 cloves
- grated ginger, one tbsp
- arrowroot powder, one tbsp
- avocado oil, one tbsp
- Broccoli slice into florets, 1 head
- freshly cracked black pepper and salt

INSTRUCTIONS:

a) Combine the coconut aminos and arrowroot powder in a dish.
b) Warm the avocado oil in a sizeable skillet or wok across high flame.
c) Stir-fry the slice flank steak till it is browned and cooked through.
d) Stir-fry the broccoli florets, minced garlic, and grated ginger till tender.
e) Stir the coconut aminos mixture, and salt and pepper into the beef and broccoli.

Turkey Meatballs with Marinara Sauce

NUTRITION: Calories 292.5|Fat 6g|Saturated Fat 1.8 g|Sodium 798.7 mg |Potassium 634.2 mg|Carbohydrate 29.2 g|Protein 31.1 g

INGREDIENTS:

- ground turkey, 1 pound
- Egg, 1
- freshly cracked black pepper and salt
- garlic powder, half tsp
- red pepper flakes, quarter tsp
- marinara sauce, one cup
- almond flour, half cup
- dried oregano, 1 tsp

INSTRUCTIONS:

a) Preset the oven to 375 degrees.
b) In a mixing dish, combine the ground turkey, almond flour, egg, garlic powder, dried oregano, and red pepper flakes.
c) Roll the mixture into small-sized meatballs and put them on a-lined baking sheet.
d) Bake the meatballs for roughly 25 mins, till all around good.
e) Cook the marinara sauce in a pot across moderate flame intensity.
f) Garnish the meatballs with the marinara sauce and season them with salt and pepper.

Beef Veggie Stew

NUTRITION: 294 Calories| 10g Fat (2g Saturated)| 84mg Cholesterol | 88mg Sodium| 16g Carbohydrates (2g fiber| 12g Sugar | 4g Added)| 32g Protein

INGREDIENTS:

- beef stew meat, 2 pounds
- tomato paste, 2 tbsps
- dried thyme, 2 tsps
- olive oil, 2 tbsps
- carrots, skinned & sliced, three
- celery stalks, sliced, three
- garlic, minced, 2 cloves
- onion, sliced, 1
- freshly cracked black pepper and salt
- low-sodium beef broth, 4 cups
- bay leaves, 2

INSTRUCTIONS:

a) Warm the olive oil inside a saucepan across moderate-high flame.
b) Sear beef stew meat till it is browned on all sides.
c) In a pot, cook onion, carrots, celery, and garlic, for 6 mins, till the vegetables are somewhat delicate and soft.
d) Include the bay leaves, thyme, tomato paste, and beef broth.
e) Raise the mixture to a rolling boil, then diminish the flame and gently simmer for about two hrs, or till the meat is tender.
f) Eliminate the bay leaves and drizzle with salt and pepper as required.

Coconut Chia Pudding

NUTRITION: 233 calories|protein 4.8g|carbohydrates 27.7g |dietary fiber10.1g|sugars 14.4g| fat 12.7g |saturated fat 1.1g|Sodium 83 mg

INGREDIENTS:

- half cup unsweetened coconut milk
- vanilla extract, half tsp
- honey or maple syrup, 1 tsp
- chia seeds, quarter cup

INSTRUCTIONS:

a) Combine the coconut milk, chia seeds, vanilla essence, and sweetener.
b) Refrigerate for at least 2 hours, preferably overnight.
c) As desired, garnish with fresh fruit or nuts.

Chocolate Avocado Pudding

NUTRITION: Calories: 462| Fat: 20.1g | Carbohydrates: 48.2g | Fiber: 10.2g | Sugars: 30.4g | Protein: 3g | Sodium: 3.5mg

INGREDIENTS:

- ripe avocados, 2
- cocoa powder, quarter cup
- almond milk, quarter cup
- honey or maple syrup, quarter cup
- vanilla extract, 1 tsp

INSTRUCTIONS:

a) Halve the avocados and eliminate the pit.
b) In a food processor, blitz half of the avocado flesh, cocoa powder, honey or maple syrup, almond milk, and vanilla extract till the mixture is smooth and creamy.
c) Refrigerate the pudding for at least 30 mins before serving.

Roasted Chickpeas

NUTRITION: 197 Calories| Protein 7.8g| Carbohydrates 24.2g | Fiber 3.7g | sugar 3.1 g | Fat 8.3g | Saturated fat 4.3g | Sodium 233mg

INGREDIENTS:

- olive oil, 1 tbsp
- freshly cracked black pepper and salt
- garlic powder, half tsp
- 1 can chickpeas, drained and rinsed
- paprika, half tsp
- cumin, half tsp

INSTRUCTIONS:

a) Preset the oven to 400 degrees F.
b) Dry the chickpeas with a paper towel.
c) Combine the salt, pepper, olive oil, garlic powder, paprika, cumin, and cumin in a small dish.
d) Coat the chickpeas thoroughly in the spice mixture.
e) On a baking sheet, spread the chickpeas out in a single layer.
f) Roast for around 25 mins, till firm and brilliant brown.

Cinnamon Roasted Almonds

NUTRITION: Calories 260 | Protein 4.4 grams|Fat 2.9 grams |Carbohydrates 40.5 grams |Sodium 77 mg

INGREDIENTS:

- cinnamon, 1 tsp
- 2 cups raw almonds
- honey, 1 tbsp
- 1 tbsp coconut oil, melted
- salt, quarter tsp

INSTRUCTIONS:

a) Set the oven to 350°F.
b) Whisk together the sweetener, melted coconut oil, cinnamon, and salt in a sizeable dish.
c) Toss the almonds in the dish till evenly covered.
d) Place the almonds in a solitary layer on a baking sheet.
e) Oven-roast for about 20 mins, till fragrant and golden brown.
f) Allow the almonds to cool completely before serving.

Apple Chips

NUTRITION: Calories: 152| Fat: 7 g | Carbohydrates: 24g | Sugar: 18g | Fiber: 5g | Protein: 1g | Sodium: 45mg

INGREDIENTS:

- apples, cored and thinly sliced, 2
- cinnamon, 1 tbsp
- Nutmeg, quarter tsp
- honey, 1 tbsp

INSTRUCTIONS:

a) Preset the oven to 225°F.
b) In a small bowl, combine the cinnamon and nutmeg.
c) Place the apple cuts on a lined baking sheet.
d) Sprinkle the apple slices with the cinnamon and nutmeg mixture.
e) Bake for around 3 hours, till the apple cuts are fresh and brilliant brown.
f) Before serving, let the apple chips cool fully.

Chocolate Peanut Butter Energy Bites

NUTRITION: Calories 254| Fat 37 g| Cholesterol 166 mg| Sodium 411 mg | Carbohydrates 73| Protein 41 g

INGREDIENTS:

- honey or maple syrup, quarter cup
- chocolate chips, quarter cup
- Rolled oats, 1 cup
- Pinch of salt
- peanut butter, half cup
- vanilla extract, 1 tsp

INSTRUCTIONS:

a) Combine the rolled oats, peanut butter, sweetener, chocolate chips, vanilla extract, and salt in a sizeable mixing dish.
b) Make tiny balls out of the mixture.
c) Arrange the balls on a prepared baking sheet.
d) Before serving, chill the energy bites for at least 30 mins.

Sweet Potato Paprika Fries

NUTRITION: Calories 460|Fat 23g grams|Saturated Fat 9g grams |Sodium 1000mg milligrams|Carbohydrates 24g grams |Protein 40g grams

INGREDIENTS:

- paprika, half tsp
- sweet potatoes peeled and slice into strips, 2
- freshly cracked black pepper and salt
- olive oil, 1 tbsp
- garlic powder, half tsp

INSTRUCTIONS:

a) Set the oven to 400°F.
b) In a sizeable dish, combine the sweet potato, olive oil, paprika, garlic, salt, and pepper.
c) Layer the sweet potato strips on a baking sheet in a singular layer.
d) Bake the sweet potato fries for 25 mins or till crispy and golden brown.

Mixed Berry Cobbler

NUTRITION: Calories 550| Total Fat 32.23 g| Saturated Fat 15.22 g | Cholesterol 61.01 mg| Sodium 3 mg |Total Carbohydrates 63.12 g| Dietary Fiber 8.97 g| Protein 743 g

INGREDIENTS:

- mixed berries, 4 cups
- cinnamon, 1 tsp
- honey or maple syrup, quarter cup
- quarter cup almond flour
- quarter cup rolled oats
- coconut oil, melted, 2 tbsps

INSTRUCTIONS:

a) Preset the oven to 375°F.
b) In a sizeable mixing dish, combine the mixed berries and honey or maple syrup.
c) Fill a baking dish halfway with the berry mixture.
d) Combine the almond flour, rolled oats, coconut oil, and cinnamon in a separate bowl till crumbly.
e) Sprinkle the berry mixture with the crumb mixture.
f) Bake for 30 mins, or till the top is brilliant brown and bubbling.
g) If desired, serve the mixed berry cobbler warm with whipped cream or vanilla ice cream.

Chocolate Banana Ice Cream

NUTRITION: Calories: 179| Fat: 16.8g | Carbs: 7.3g | Fiber: 2.4g | Sugars: 2.9g | Protein: 3.4g | Sodium: 120.5mg

INGREDIENTS:

- cocoa powder, 2 tbsps
- 2 ripe bananas, sliced and frozen
- honey, 1 tbsp
- vanilla extract, half tsp

INSTRUCTIONS:

a) Blend the frozen banana slices, cocoa powder, honey or maple syrup, and vanilla extract till smooth and creamy.
b) Immediately serve the chocolate banana ice cream.

WEEK 3: CONVERSION

Week 3 of Metabolic Flexibility focuses on converting the body to a state of metabolic flexibility. This week includes meals and snacks that are designed to shift the body from relying on carbohydrates as the primary fuel source to being able to efficiently use both carbohydrates and fats for energy.

The body's capacity to transform one type of macronutrient into another to generate energy is referred to as conversion, which is another crucial principle of metabolic flexibility. To ensure that the body has a consistent supply of fuel and maintains energy homeostasis, this conversion process is necessary.

The process of gluconeogenesis, in which the body converts non-carbohydrate sources like amino acids and glycerol into glucose for energy production, is one example of macronutrient conversion. This cycle happens basically in the liver and is basic for keeping up with blood glucose levels during times of fasting or sugar limitation.

The process of de novo lipogenesis, in which the body converts excess carbohydrates into fatty acids that are stored as triglycerides, is another example of macronutrient conversion. This process is necessary for storing excess energy for later use and takes place primarily in the liver and adipose tissue.

Scrambled eggs with avocado and spinach

NUTRITION: Calories:203| Fat: 17 g | Carbohydrates: 2 Fiber: 1 g | Protein: 13g|Sodium 278.3 mg

INGREDIENTS:

- 2 eggs
- half avocado, diced
- half cup spinach leaves
- freshly cracked black pepper and salt

INSTRUCTIONS:

a) Whisk the eggs well along with salt and pepper.
b) Cook the egg mixture in a nonstick skillet over moderate heat for about 3 mins, or till the eggs are firm.
c) Include spinach and cook for an additional 2 mins, or till the spinach is shriveled.
d) Serve immediately with diced avocado on top.

Oatmeal with nuts and seeds

NUTRITION: Calories: 121| Fat: 3.2g | Carbohydrates: 17.8g | Fiber: 3g | Sugars: 2.5g | Protein: 3.9g|Sodium 95 mg

INGREDIENTS:

- rolled oats, half cup
- Water
- chia seeds, 1 tbsp
- hemp seeds, 1 tbsp
- almond butter, 1 tbsp
- mixed nuts, quarter cup

INSTRUCTIONS:

a) Bring a cup of water to a boil in a saucepan.
b) Lower the heat and include the oats while stirring.
c) Cook the oats for about 6 mins, stirring in between, or till they are soft.
d) Stir in the chia seeds, hemp seeds, and almond butter till completely combined.
e) Serve hot, garnished with sliced nuts.

Banana pancakes

NUTRITION: Calories Per Serving: 290 |Fat 19g|Cholesterol 0mg |Sodium 10mg|Carbohydrates 28g|Sugars 18g|Protein 6g

INGREDIENTS:

- 1 ripe banana, mashed
- Butter or oil for cooking
- 2 eggs
- baking powder, quarter tsp
- vanilla extract, quarter tsp

INSTRUCTIONS:

a) Combine the mashed banana, baking powder, eggs, and vanilla extract in a dish.
b) In a nonstick skillet over moderate heat intensity, melt butter or oil.
c) Ladle in batter and cook for around 3 mins per side till golden brown.
d) Repeat with the rest of the batter.
e) Serve immediately.

Breakfast burrito

NUTRITION: Calories 465 | Fat 15 g | Saturated fat 2.8 g |Sodium 856 mg | Carbohydrate 73 g | fiber 6 g |Sugar 0.5 g |Protein 9 g

INGREDIENTS:

- Eggs, 2
- shredded cheddar cheese, quarter cup
- whole wheat tortillas, 2
- black beans, quarter cup
- avocado, sliced, quarter

INSTRUCTIONS:

a) Scramble the eggs in a nonstick skillet over moderate heat intensity.
b) Warm the whole wheat tortillas and black beans.
c) Fill every tortilla with scrambled eggs, black beans, avocado, and shredded cheddar cheese.
d) Roll the tortilla into a burrito shape. Serve hot.

Green smoothie

NUTRITION: Calories 74|Total Fat 0.5g| Carbohydrates 13g|Protein 1g | Sodium 39mg

INGREDIENTS:

- Banana, 1
- spinach leaves, 1 cup
- unsweetened almond milk, half cup
- Greek yogurt, quarter cup
- honey, 1 tbsp

INSTRUCTIONS:

a) Blend the banana, spinach leaves, almond milk, Greek yogurt, and honey till completely smooth.
b) Chill before serving.

Spinach and feta omelet

NUTRITION: Calories: 284| Fat: 19.1g | Carbohydrates: 16g | Fiber: 3.1g | Sugars: 12.5g | Protein: 12.9g|Sodium 33 mg

INGREDIENTS:

- Eggs, 2
- baby spinach leaves, quarter cup
- crumbled feta cheese, quarter cup
- freshly cracked black pepper and salt
- Butter, 1 tbsp

INSTRUCTIONS:

a) Whisk the eggs in a dish and drizzle with salt and pepper.
b) In a nonstick skillet, melt the butter over moderate heat.
c) Cook the spinach leaves in the skillet for 2 mins, till shriveled.
d) In a skillet, cook the whisked eggs for two mins.
e) Top with feta cheese.
f) Fold the omelet in half utilizing a spatula.
g) Serve right away.

Breakfast quinoa bowl

NUTRITION: Calories: 248 | Fat: 11.4g | Carbohydrates: 30.5g | Fiber: 4.4g | Sugars: 1.3g | Protein: 7.4g|Sodium 34.5 mg

INGREDIENTS:

- cooked quinoa, 1 cup
- half cup sliced strawberries
- quarter cup sliced almonds
- honey, 1 tbsp
- cinnamon, half tsp

INSTRUCTIONS:

a) Combine the cooked quinoa, sliced strawberries, sliced almonds, honey, and cinna mon in a mixing dish.
b) To blend, stir everything together thoroughly.
c) Serve warm or cold.

Cheesy Breakfast frittata

NUTRITION: Calories:203| Fat: 17 g | Carbohydrates: 2 Fiber: 1 g | Protein: 13g|Sodium 278.3 mg

INGREDIENTS:

- Eggs, 6
- sliced vegetables (such as spinach, bell peppers, onions, or mushrooms), half cup
- shredded cheese, quarter cup
- freshly cracked black pepper and salt
- olive oil, 1 tbsp

INSTRUCTIONS:

a) Set the oven to 350°F.
b) Heat the olive oil in a nonstick skillet over moderate heat.
c) Include veggies and cook for roughly 4 mins, till the vegetables are tender.
d) In a dish, whisk together the eggs and drizzle with salt and pepper.
e) Place the eggs in the skillet with the vegetables.
f) Sprinkle some cheese on top.
g) Bake for 13 mins, or till the cheese has melted and the frittata is firm.
h) Serve right away.

Grilled chicken wrap

NUTRITION: Calories 455 | Fat 15 g | Saturated fat 3 g |Sodium 856 mg | Carbohydrate 73 g | fiber 6 g |Sugar 1 g |Protein 11 g

INGREDIENTS:

- grilled chicken breast, sliced, 4 ounces
- whole wheat tortilla, 1
- mixed greens, quarter cup
- cucumber, sliced, quarter cup
- cherry tomatoes, halved, quarter cup
- Greek yogurt, 1 tbsp

INSTRUCTIONS:

a) On the whole wheat tortilla, spread the Greek yogurt.
b) Combine the grilled chicken, mixed greens, cucumber, and cherry tomatoes in a dish.
c) Wrap the tortilla in a towel.
d) Chill before serving.

Tuna salad sandwich

NUTRITION: Calories 326 | 45g Fats | 5g Carbohydrates | 39g Protein | 700mg Sodium

INGREDIENTS:

- 4 ounces canned tuna, drained
- Greek yogurt, quarter cup
- Diced celery, quarter cup
- Dijon mustard, 1 tbsp
- freshly cracked black pepper and salt
- whole wheat bread, 2 slices
- mixed greens, half cup

INSTRUCTIONS:

a) Combine the canned tuna, Dijon mustard, salt, Greek yogurt, celery, and pepper in a dish.
b) Stir everything together thoroughly.
c) Toast the whole wheat bread and spread one slice with tuna salad.
d) Top with the mixed greens and the remaining slice of bread.
e) Chill before serving.

Chickpea and vegetable stir-fry

NUTRITION: Calories: 215 | Fat: 7 g | Saturated Fat: 1.0 g | Sodium: 128 Mg | Carbohydrate: 36 g | Dietary Fiber: 9 g | Sugar: 14 g | Protein: 7 g

INGREDIENTS:

- olive oil, 2 tbsps
- chickpeas, drained and rinsed, 1 can
- mixed vegetables (such as bell peppers, onions, and broccoli), 1 cup
- cumin, 1 tsp
- chili powder, half tsp
- freshly cracked black pepper and salt

INSTRUCTIONS:

a) Heat the olive oil in a skillet over moderate-high heat.
b) Cook mixed vegetables and chickpeas for around 6 mins, till the vegetables are delicately soft.
c) Sprinkle with cumin, chili powder, salt, and pepper.
d) Serve immediately.

Black bean and Sweet potato tacos

NUTRITION: Calories 460|Fat 23g grams|Saturated Fat 9g grams |Sodium 1000mg milligrams|Carbohydrates 24g grams |Protein 40g grams

INGREDIENTS:

- corn tortillas, 4
- small sweet potatoes, diced, 2
- freshly cracked black pepper and salt
- black beans, drained and rinsed, 1 can
- cilantro, sliced, quarter cup
- lime, juiced, 1
- red onion, diced, quarter cup

INSTRUCTIONS:

a) Set the oven to 400°F.
b) On a baking sheet, roast the diced sweet potatoes for about 25 mins, or till they are soft.
c) In a dish, combine the black beans, cilantro, red onion, lime juice, salt, and pepper.
d) In the oven or on the stovetop, warm the corn tortillas.
e) To the tortillas, include the roasted sweet potatoes and black bean mixture.
f) Serve immediately.

Turkey and vegetable wrap

NUTRITION: Calories 292.5|Fat 6g|Saturated Fat 1.8 g|Sodium 798.7 mg |Potassium 634.2 mg|Carbohydrate 29.2 g|Protein 31.1 g

INGREDIENTS:

- deli turkey, 2 ounces
- whole wheat tortilla, 1
- mixed greens, quarter cup
- cucumber, sliced, quarter cup
- cherry tomatoes, halved, quarter cup
- Hummus, 1 tbsp

INSTRUCTIONS:

a) On the whole wheat tortilla, spread the hummus.
b) Combine the deli turkey, mixed greens, cucumber, and cherry tomatoes in a dish.
c) Wrap the tortilla in a towel.
d) Chill before serving.

Broiled salmon with quinoa and roasted vegetables

NUTRITION: Calories 330 |Fat 17.7g| Saturated fat 2.6g|Polyunsaturated fat 5.6|Cholesterol 109.1mg|Sodium 126.5mg |Carbohydrates 1g|Sugar 0g| Fiber 0.4g|Protein 39.5g

INGREDIENTS:

- olive oil, 1 tbsp
- salmon fillet, 4 ounces
- cooked quinoa, half cup
- mixed roasted vegetables (such as broccoli, cauliflower, and carrots), 1 cup
- freshly cracked black pepper and salt

INSTRUCTIONS:

a) Set the oven to broil.
b) Season both sides of the salmon fillet with salt and pepper.
c) Cook on broil for about 6 mins, or till thoroughly cooked.
d) Combine the cooked quinoa and roasted vegetables in a mixing dish.
e) Sprinkle the quinoa and vegetables with salt and pepper after drizzling with olive oil.
f) Serve immediately.

Grilled shrimp and vegetable kebabs

NUTRITION: Calories 12|Fat 0.3g grams|Saturated Fat 0.1g grams |Carbohydrates 0.5g grams|Fiber 0.1g grams |Sugars 0.1g grams|Protein 1.3g| Sodium 75mg

INGREDIENTS:

- shrimp, peeled and deveined, 8 ounces
- yellow squash, sliced, 1
- red onion, diced small, 1
- freshly cracked black pepper and salt
- balsamic vinegar, 2 tbsps
- olive oil, 2 tbsps
- Sliced zucchini, 1
- Diced red bell pepper, 1
- Diced green bell pepper, 1
- dried oregano, 1 tsp

INSTRUCTIONS:

a) Submerge wooden skewers in water for at least 30 mins.
b) Thread the shrimp and vegetables onto the skewers.
c) Whisk the salt, pepper, balsamic vinegar, dried oregano, and olive oil together.
d) Use the glaze mixture to brush the skewers.
e) Grill the sticks for around 4 mins on every side.
f) Serve right away.

Baked salmon with asparagus and lemon

NUTRITION: Calories 344 |Fat 18| Saturated fat 3g|Sodium 126mg |Carbohydrates 1g|Protein 39.5g

INGREDIENTS:

- salmon fillet, 4 ounces
- Asparagus, half bunch
- Sliced lemon, 1
- olive oil, 2 tbsps
- freshly cracked black pepper and salt

INSTRUCTIONS:

a) Preset the oven to 400°F.
b) Sprinkle salmon fillet with salt and pepper and place in the center of an aluminum foil sheet.
c) Arrange asparagus spears and lemon slices around the salmon.
d) Over the salmon, asparagus, and lemon, drizzle the olive oil. Form a pouch out of the foil.
e) Bake salmon and asparagus for around 20 mins, till the salmon is cooked through.
f) Serve immediately.

Turkey chili

NUTRITION: Calories 292.5|Fat 6g|Saturated Fat 1.8 g|Sodium 798.7 mg |Potassium 634.2 mg|Carbohydrate 29.2 g|Protein 31.1 g

INGREDIENTS:

- Minced garlic, 2 cloves
- diced tomatoes, undrained, 14-ounce can
- sliced onion, 1
- Sliced red bell pepper, 1
- sliced green bell pepper, 1
- kidney beans drained and rinsed, 15-ounce can
- ground turkey, 1 pound
- chili powder, 1 tbsp
- freshly cracked black pepper and salt

INSTRUCTIONS:

a) Heat a sizeable saucepan to a moderate-high temperature.
b) Include the turkey and cook for about 6 mins, or till the turkey is browned.
c) Include the diced onion, red pepper, green pepper, and garlic.
d) Cook the vegetables for another 5 mins, or till they are tender.
e) To the pot, include the diced tomatoes (undrained), kidney beans, chili powder, salt, and pepper.
f) Bring to a rolling boil, then gently simmer on low heat for around 25 mins.
g) Serve immediately.

Grilled steak with roasted sweet potatoes

NUTRITION: Calories 296| Total Fat 16g| Saturated Fat 5.9g| Trans Fat 0.6g | Polyunsaturated Fat 1g| Monounsaturated Fat 6.4g | Cholesterol 103mg| Sodium 639mg

INGREDIENTS:

- dried rosemary, 1 tsp
- sirloin steak, 4 ounces
- sweet potato peeled and cubed, 1
- freshly cracked black pepper and salt
- olive oil, 1 tbsp

INSTRUCTIONS:

a) Set the oven to 400°F.
b) Toss the cubes of sweet potato with olive oil, dried rosemary, salt, and pepper.
c) On a baking sheet, layer the sweet potatoes in a single layer.
d) Roast for around 25 mins, till soft and tender.
e) Season the steak well with salt and pepper.
f) Grill the steak for around 4 mins per side on high heat for moderate-rare, or you can grill for a longer time to your preference.
g) Serve immediately with roasted sweet potatoes.

Grilled pork chops with roasted vegetables

NUTRITION: Calories: 130| Fat: 11.1g | Carbohydrates: 6.1g | Fiber: 2.3g | Sugars: 2.9g | Protein: 3.3g | Sodium: 45mg

INGREDIENTS:

- bone-in pork chops, 2
- red onion, slice into wedges, 1
- sweet potato peeled and cubed, 1
- olive oil, 2 tbsps
- Brussels sprouts, halved, half pound
- dried thyme, 1 tsp
- freshly cracked black pepper and salt

INSTRUCTIONS:

a) Set the oven to 400°F.
b) Toss the Brussels sprouts, red onion, and sweet potato with olive oil, dried thyme, salt, and pepper in a sizeable dish.
c) Place the vegetables in a single layer on a baking sheet.
d) Roast for around 25 mins, till tender and lightly browned.
e) Sprinkle salt and pepper thoroughly over the pork chops.
f) Grill the pork chops on high heat intensity for around 4 mins per side for moderate-rare, till cooked to your liking.
g) Serve immediately with the roasted vegetables.

Chicken and vegetable curry

NUTRITION: 233 calories| 6g fat (1g saturated fat)|70mg cholesterol | 866mg sodium| 13g carbohydrate (0 sugars, 3g fiber) | 33g protein

INGREDIENTS:

- Boneless skinless chicken breast, cubed, 4 ounces
- coconut milk, 14-ounce can
- onion, sliced, 1
- Minced garlic, 2 cloves
- freshly cracked black pepper and salt
- red bell pepper, sliced, 1
- yellow squash, cubed, 1
- red curry paste, 2 tbsps

INSTRUCTIONS:

a) Melt the butter in a sizeable skillet over moderate-high heat.
b) In the skillet, cook the cubed chicken for roughly 6 mins, till sautéed.
c) In the skillet, include the diced red bell pepper, yellow squash, sliced onion, and minced garlic.
d) Cook the vegetables for another 5 mins till they are tender.
e) In the skillet, include the red curry paste and coconut milk.
f) Bring to a gentle boil and then cook on a simmer for 13 mins, till the sauce has thickened fairly.
g) Sprinkle with one pinch every of pepper and salt.
h) Serve immediately over quinoa or rice.

Spaghetti squash with meat sauce

NUTRITION: 195 Calories| Protein 7.8g| Carbohydrates 24.2g | Fiber 3.7g | Sugar 2.1 g | Fat 8.3g | Saturated fat 4.3g | Sodium 849.0mg

INGREDIENTS:

- spaghetti squash, 1
- lean ground beef, 1 pound
- dried oregano, 1 tsp
- diced tomatoes, 14-ounce can
- tomato paste, 2 tbsps
- freshly cracked black pepper and salt
- Sliced onion, 1
- Minced garlic, 2 cloves

INSTRUCTIONS:

a) Set the oven to 375°F.
b) Scoop the seeds out of the spaghetti squash after cutting it in half along its length.
c) Place the slice sides down of the squash halves on a baking sheet.
d) Bake the squash till it is tender, about 35 mins.
e) While the squash cooks, brown the ground beef in a sizeable skillet over moderate-high intensity.
f) In the skillet, include the minced garlic and sliced onion.
g) Simmer the onion for about 6 mins, or till it becomes transparent.
h) In the skillet, include the diced tomatoes, tomato paste, dried oregano, salt, and pepper.
i) Combine everything by stirring.
j) Cook the meat sauce over moderate heat for 13 mins, or till it starts to thicken.
k) Using a fork, scrape the spaghetti squash strands into a bowl.
l) Serve the beef sauce over the squash strands.

Blueberry Oat Bars

NUTRITION: Calories: 170| 3g Fat| 171mg Sodium| 30g Carbohydrates (4g fiber| 15g Sugar| 7g Added)| 7g Protein

INGREDIENTS:

- brown sugar, half cup
- oats, 1 cup
- unsalted butter, melted, half cup
- egg, 1, lightly beaten
- baking soda, half tsp
- salt, half tsp
- all-purpose flour, 1 cup
- Blueberries, 1 cup

INSTRUCTIONS:

a) Set the oven to 350ºF.
b) Combine the oats, flour, brown sugar, baking soda, and salt in a sizeable dish.
c) Include the beaten egg and the melted butter.
d) Stir the mixture till it is well-combined.
e) Combine in the blueberries.
f) Put half of the mixture in a baking dish that is 8 inches square.
g) Bake for about 28 mins, or till the top is golden brown.
h) Before cutting the bars into squares, allow them to completely cool.

Peanut Butter and Jelly Energy Bites

NUTRITION: 233 calories| protein 4.8g|carbohydrates 27.7g |dietary fiber10.1g|sugars 14.4g| fat 12.7g|saturated fat 1.1g |Sodium 83 mg

INGREDIENTS:

- natural peanut butter, half cup
- Honey, quarter cup
- vanilla extract, 1 tsp
- old-fashioned oats, 1quarter cups
- dried cranberries, quarter cup
- Raisins, quarter cup
- sliced nuts, quarter cup
- Salt, 1 pinch
- chia seeds, quarter cup

INSTRUCTIONS:

a) Combine the peanut butter, honey, and vanilla extract in a moderate dish.
b) Combine the oats, dried cranberries, raisins, sliced almonds, chia seeds, and salt in another dish.
c) Stir the components together thoroughly.
d) Form the mixture into little balls using your hands.
e) Refrigerate the energy balls for 30 mins or more before serving, on a plate or baking sheet.

Apple Crisp

NUTRITION: Calories: 161| Fat: 0.6g | Carbohydrates: 41.6g | Fiber: 5.6g | Sugars: 33.1g | Protein: 1.7g | Sodium: 8mg

INGREDIENTS:

- cinnamon, half tsp
- sliced apples, 4 cups
- all-purpose flour, half cup
- rolled oats, half cup
- brown sugar, half cup
- melted butter, half cup

INSTRUCTIONS:

a) Preset the oven to 350 °F and grease an 8x8-inch baking dish.
b) In a sizeable mixing bowl, combine the brown sugar, cinnamon, flour, oats, and sliced apples.
c) After thoroughly mixing the components, pour the melted butter over them.
d) Pour the prepared mixture into the baking dish you prepared.
e) Bake for 35 mins, or till the apples are tender and the top is golden brown.
f) Serve warm apple crisp with vanilla ice cream.

Chocolate Chip Banana Bread

NUTRITION: Calories: 369| Fat: 22.5g | Carbohydrates: 31g | Fiber: 10.8g | Sugars: 8.8 g | Protein: 14.1g|Sodium 370 mg

INGREDIENTS:

- all-purpose flour, 2 cups
- unsalted softened butter, half cup
- Mashed ripe bananas, 3
- semisweet chocolate chips, 1 cup
- Sugar, 1 cup
- baking soda, 1 tsp
- salt, quarter tsp
- Eggs, 2
- vanilla extract, 1 tsp

INSTRUCTIONS:

a) Set the oven to 350°F.
b) Using cooking spray, grease a 9x5-inch loaf pan.
c) Combine the salt, baking soda, and flour in a dish. In a sizeable blending dish, blend the melted margarine or butter and sugar.
d) Include the vanilla extract and eggs. Include the mashed bananas.
e) Stir the dry fixings into the fluid fixings gently till well combined.
f) Include the chocolate chips and combine.
g) Pour the batter into the loaf pan that you previously prepared.
h) Bake the bread for 65 mins, or till a toothpick inserted into the center comes out clean.
i) Cool before slicing and serving the banana bread.

Almond Butter Chocolate Chip Cookies

NUTRITION: Calories 160 |Fat 12g |Saturated fat 4.5g|Sodium 60mg |Carbohydrates 12g |Sugar 8g |Fiber 3g |Protein 3g

INGREDIENTS:

- baking soda, half tsp
- salt, quarter tsp
- almond butter, half cup
- Egg, 1
- vanilla extract, 1 tsp
- brown sugar, half cup
- semisweet chocolate chips, half cup

INSTRUCTIONS:

a) Set the oven to 350°F.
b) In a dish, combine the egg, vanilla essence, brown sugar, and almond butter.
c) Combine in the salt and baking soda thoroughly. Include the chocolate chips by hand.
d) Roll the dough into 1-inch balls and set them on a parchment-lined baking sheet.
e) Press down on the balls to straighten them somewhat.
f) Cook for nine mins, or till the edges begin to brown.
g) After the cookies have cooled completely on the baking sheet for five mins, transfer them to a wire rack.

Chocolate Zucchini Bread

NUTRITION: Calories: 374| Fat: 15.8g | Carbohydrates: 30.8g | Fiber: 5.2g | Sugars: 16.8 g | Protein: 31g | Sodium: 113.2mg

INGREDIENTS:

- salt, half tsp
- unsalted softened butter, half cup
- baking soda, 1 tsp
- all-purpose flour, 1half cups
- unsweetened cocoa powder, half cup
- granulated sugar, half cup
- Eggs, 2
- vanilla extract, 1 tsp
- Greek yogurt, half cup
- shredded zucchini, 1half cups
- chocolate chips, half cup
- baking powder, half tsp
- brown sugar, half cup

INSTRUCTIONS:

a) Set the oven to 350 °Fand grease a 9x5-inch loaf pan.
b) In a dish, combine the flour, cocoa powder, baking soda, baking powder, and salt.
c) In another bowl, cream together the melted butter, and both sugars.
d) Combine in the eggs and vanilla extract.
e) Include the Greek yogurt.
f) Gently fold the dry components into the liquid components till just mixed.
g) Include the shredded zucchini and chocolate chips.
h) Fill the prepared loaf pan halfway with the batter.
i) Bake the bread in the oven for about an hour, or till a toothpick inserted in the center comes out clean.
j) Allow to cool before slicing and serving the zucchini bread.

Coconut Macaroons

NUTRITION: 233 calories| 6g fat (1g saturated fat) |70mg cholesterol | 866mg sodium| 13g carbohydrate (0 sugars, 3g fiber) | 33g protein

INGREDIENTS:

- sweetened shredded coconut, 2half cups
- sweetened condensed milk, ⅔ cup
- 2 egg whites
- vanilla extract, 1 tsp
- Pinch of salt

INSTRUCTIONS:

a) Set the oven to 350°F.
b) Using parchment paper, Prepare a baking sheet.
c) In a dish, include the vanilla essence, shredded coconut, sweetened condensed milk, and salt.
d) Separately, whisk the egg whites till stiff peaks form.
e) Fold in the beaten egg whites till completely mixed with the coconut mixture.
f) Drop the mixture onto the prepared baking sheet using a small cookie scoop, spacing it about an inch apart.
g) Bake for about 14 mins, till the edges have a light golden color.
h) After the macaroons have cooled completely on the baking sheet for five mins, transfer them to a wire rack.

WEEK 4: RHYTHM

Week 4 of Metabolic Flexibility focuses on establishing a rhythm of eating that supports metabolic flexibility. This week includes meals and snacks that are designed to support the body's natural circadian rhythms and optimize digestion and nutrient absorption.

Rhythm is the body's natural cyclical patterns of energy metabolism, which is another principle of metabolic flexibility. The circadian rhythm, which is the 24-hour cycle of physiological processes that regulate sleep, hormone production, and metabolism, is one of the most important rhythms in metabolism.

Another important aspect of rhythm regulation is meal timing. Intermittent fasting or time-restricted eating can promote metabolic flexibility by allowing the body to switch between fat and carbohydrate metabolism while eating at regular intervals throughout the day can aid in controlling insulin and blood glucose levels.

To promote metabolic flexibility and maintain overall health and wellness, understanding rhythm is essential. By supporting normal rhythms through customary dinner timing, exercise, and rest propensities, people can advance Metabolic flexibility and lessen the chances of metabolic problems.

Shakshuka

NUTRITION: Calories: 284| Fat: 19.1g | Carbohydrates: 16g | Fiber: 3.1g | Sugars: 12.5g | Protein: 12.9g|Sodium 33 mg

INGREDIENTS:

- diced tomatoes, 14.5-ounce can
- Sliced red bell pepper, 1
- Eggs, 6
- freshly cracked black pepper and salt
- Minced garlic, 2 cloves
- ground cumin, 1 tsp
- paprika, half tsp
- cayenne pepper, quarter tsp
- olive oil, 2 tbsps
- Sliced onion, 1
- Fresh parsley, sliced, for garnish

INSTRUCTIONS:

a) Warm the olive oil in a sizeable skillet over moderate heat intensity.
b) In about 5 mins, cook the bell pepper and onion till soft.
c) After adding the garlic, cumin, paprika, and cayenne pepper, cook for one more moment.
d) Simmer for ten mins, or till the sauce thickens, before adding the diced tomatoes.
e) Place an egg in every of the tomato sauce's small wells made with a spoon.
f) Cover the skillet and cook the eggs for six mins, or till the way you like them done.
g) drizzle with salt and pepper before serving, and decorate with fresh parsley.

Sweet Potato Hash with Eggs

NUTRITION: Calories 460|Fat 23g grams|Saturated Fat 9g grams |Sodium 1000mg milligrams|Carbohydrates 24g grams |Fiber 4g grams|Sugars 7g grams|Protein 40g grams

INGREDIENTS:

- ground cumin, 1 tsp
- olive oil, 2 tbsps
- freshly cracked black pepper and salt
- sweet potatoes peeled and diced, 2
- smoked paprika, 1 tsp
- Eggs, 6
- Sliced onion, 1
- Minced garlic, 2 cloves
- Fresh cilantro, sliced, for garnish

INSTRUCTIONS:

a) In a sizeable skillet, heat the olive oil to a moderate temperature.
b) Pan-fry the sweet potatoes, onion, garlic, cumin, and smoky paprika for about ten mins, or till they are tender.
c) Crack the eggs into the skillet and cover it.
d) Cook them for about 6 mins, or till the way you like them done.
e) Before serving, drizzle with fresh cilantro and drizzle with salt and pepper to taste.

Chorizo and Vegetable Frittata

NUTRITION: Calories:203| Fat: 17 g | Carbohydrates: 2 Fiber: 1 g | Protein: 13g|Sodium 278.3 mg

INGREDIENTS:

- olive oil, 1 tbsp
- red bell pepper, sliced, 1
- frozen spinach, thawed, half cup
- Eggs, 8
- shredded cheddar cheese, half cup
- freshly cracked black pepper and salt
- Milk, quarter cup
- sliced onion, half cup
- chorizo, diced, 4 ounces

INSTRUCTIONS:

a) Preset the oven to 375 °F(190 degrees Celsius).
b) Heat the olive oil in an oven-safe skillet over moderate heat till it's warm.
c) Soften the onion and bell pepper by cooking them for five mins in the skillet.
d) Brown the chorizo by cooking it for around six mins while stirring occasionally.
e) Whisk together the eggs, milk, salt, and pepper in a sizeable bowl.
f) Include the egg mixture, veggies, and chorizo to the skillet.
g) Sprinkle shredded cheddar cheese over the frittata.
h) Bake the frittata in the oven for around 18 mins till the eggs are fully cooked and the cheese is melted.

Salmon and Avocado Toast

NUTRITION: Calories: 313| Fat: 18.3g | Carbs: 1.4g | Fiber: 0.1g| Sugars: 1g | Protein: 34g| Sodium: 542.9mg

INGREDIENTS:

- whole grain bread, 2 slices
- smoked salmon, 6 ounces
- Capers, 1 tbsp
- sliced fresh dill, 1 tbsp
- avocado, sliced, 1
- freshly cracked black pepper and salt

INSTRUCTIONS:

a) Toast the bread slices to your preferred crispiness.
b) Top every slice with smoked salmon and avocado slices.
c) Sprinkle capers, dill, salt, and pepper on top of the toast.
d) Serve right away.

Cashew, and Asparagus Stir-Fry with Cauliflower Rice

NUTRITION: Calories 160| Fat 3g (Saturated 0g) | Cholesterol 0mg | Sodium 549mg| Carbohydrate 30g| Dietary Fiber 5g | Protein 8g.

INGREDIENTS:

FOR THE STIR-FRY:

- olive oil, 2 tbsps
- 1 tbsp rice vinegar
- honey, 1 tbsp
- 2 cloves garlic, minced
- asparagus, trimmed and diced, 1 pound
- half cup unsalted cashews
- 1 tbsp fresh ginger, grated
- soy sauce, 2 tbsps
- 1 tbsp cornstarch
- water, quarter cup

FOR THE CAULIFLOWER RICE:

- freshly cracked black pepper and salt
- Riced cauliflower, 1 head
- soy sauce, 2 tbsps
- butter, 2 tbsps

INSTRUCTIONS:

a) Heat the olive oil in a sizeable skillet.
b) Include the asparagus and cook till it's tender, for about 6 mins.
c) Include cashews, garlic, and ginger, and cook for an additional 2 mins.
d) In a small bowl, whisk together soy sauce, rice vinegar, honey, cornstarch, and water till smooth.
e) Include the mixture to the skillet and stir till the sauce thickens and the asparagus is coated. Cook for 2 more mins.
f) In a separate skillet, melt butter over moderate-high heat to prepare the cauliflower rice.
g) Include riced cauliflower to the skillet.
h) Include soy sauce and drizzle with freshly cracked black pepper and salt.
i) Cook the cauliflower rice for about 6 mins or till it's tender, stirring occasionally.
j) Serve the stir-fry over the butter-soy cauliflower rice.

Mediterranean Quinoa Salad

NUTRITION: 250 Calories| 9g Fat (4g Saturated)| 17mg Cholesterol | 262mg Sodium| 33g Carbohydrates (5g fiber| 4g Sugar | 0g Added)| 9g Protein

INGREDIENTS:

- cherry tomatoes, halved, half cup
- Kalamata olives, sliced, quarter cup
- olive oil, 2 tbsps
- fresh mint, 2 tbsps
- crumbled feta cheese, quarter cup
- fresh parsley, 2 tbsps
- red wine vinegar, 1 tbsp
- red bell pepper sliced, half
- Quinoa, 1 cup
- cucumber sliced, half
- red onion, sliced, half
- freshly cracked black pepper and salt

INSTRUCTIONS:

a) Cook the quinoa as per the instructions on the package and set it aside to cool.
b) Combine the quinoa, cucumber, red onion, red bell pepper, cherry tomatoes, Kalamata olives, feta cheese, parsley, and mint in a sizeable mixing dish.
c) Combine the olive oil, red wine vinegar, salt, and pepper in a small bowl and whisk together.
d) Toss the salad with the dressing till it's evenly coated.
e) Chill before serving.

Sweet Potato and Black Bean Burrito Bowl

NUTRITION: Calories 460|Fat 23g grams| Saturated Fat 9g grams | Sodium 1000mg milligrams| Carbohydrates 24g grams | Protein 40g grams

INGREDIENTS:

- cooked brown rice, 1 cup
- avocado, sliced, half
- sliced fresh cilantro, 2 tbsps
- lime juice, 1 tbsp
- red onion, sliced, half
- red bell pepper sliced, half
- sweet potato, diced, 1
- black beans rinsed and drained, 1 can
- olive oil, 1 tbsp
- freshly cracked black pepper and salt

INSTRUCTIONS:

a) Preset the oven to 400°F.
b) Sprinkle salt and pepper over the diced sweet potato on a baking sheet.
c) Roast the vegetables for 25 mins or till they become tender.
d) In a sizeable bowl, combine the cooked brown rice, black beans, red onion, red bell pepper, roasted sweet potato, cilantro, olive oil, lime juice, salt, and pepper.
e) Distribute the mixture evenly among the bowls and include avocado slices on top.
f) Serve the bowls immediately.

Chicken Skewers with Carrot and Walnut Salad

NUTRITION: Calories: 386| Fat: 11.5g | Carbohydrates: 27.4g | Fiber: 1.9g | Sugars: 24.3g | Protein: 43.6g |Sodium 174 mg

INGREDIENTS:

FOR THE CHICKEN SKEWERS:

- boneless, skinless chicken breasts, cubed, 1 pound
- yellow bell pepper, diced small, 1
- zucchini, diced small, 1
- olive oil, quarter cup
- freshly cracked black pepper and salt
- dried basil, 1 tbsp
- Minced garlic, 2 cloves
- red bell pepper, diced small, 1
- dried oregano, 1 tbsp
- red onion, diced small, 1

FOR THE CARROT AND WALNUT SALAD:

- lemon juice, 1 tbsp
- sliced walnuts, half cup
- carrots shaved into ribbons, 2
- olive oil, 2 tbsps
- sliced fresh parsley, quarter cup
- crumbled feta cheese, quarter cup
- freshly cracked black pepper and salt

INSTRUCTIONS:

a) Preset the grill or grill pan to moderate-high heat.
b) In a sizeable bowl, combine chicken, onion, peppers, zucchini, olive oil, oregano, basil, garlic, salt, and pepper.
c) Toss the chicken and vegetables to coat them evenly.
d) Thread the chicken and vegetables onto skewers, alternating them.
e) Grill the skewers for around 9 mins, turning occasionally, till the chicken is thoroughly cooked and the vegetables are tender and slightly browned.
f) While the skewers are grilling, prepare the carrot and walnut salad by combining shaved carrots, walnuts, feta cheese, parsley, olive oil, lemon juice, salt, and pepper in a bowl.
g) Toss the components well.
h) Serve the hot chicken skewers with the carrot and walnut salad.

Deconstructed Egg Roll

NUTRITION: Calories: 167|Fat: 5g|Saturated: 1g|Carbohydrate: 23g |Fiber: 3g|Protein: 6g | Sodium: 821mg

INGREDIENTS:

- ground pork, 1 pound
- green cabbage, thinly sliced, half head
- Shredded carrot, 1
- Sliced onion, 1
- Minced garlic, 3 cloves
- rice vinegar, 1 tsp
- grated ginger, 1 tbsp
- soy sauce, 2 tbsps
- sesame oil, 1 tsp
- freshly cracked black pepper and salt
- sliced green onions for garnish

INSTRUCTIONS:

a) Brown the ground pork in a sizeable skillet till it's thoroughly done. Place aside.
b) Place the same skillet over moderate heat and include the sliced onion, garlic, and ginger.
c) Cook the onions till they become tender a few mins.
d) Include the sliced cabbage and carrot to the skillet and continue to sauté till the cabbage wilts.
e) Put the cooked pork and vegetables back into the skillet.
f) Include the soy sauce, sesame oil, rice vinegar, salt, and pepper to the mixture of meat and veggies and stir well.
g) Serve hot, garnished with sliced green onions.

Chickpea and Spinach Curry

NUTRITION: Calories: 476| Fat: 24.4g | Carbohydrates: 51.3g | Fiber: 14.8g | Sugars: 11.7g | Protein: 19.2g|Sodium 174 mg

INGREDIENTS:

- coconut oil, 1 tbsp
- curry powder, 1 tbsp
- chickpeas, rinsed and drained, 1 can
- diced tomatoes, 1 can
- vegetable broth1 cup
- Sliced onion, half
- minced garlic, 2 cloves
- spinach leaves, 3 cups
- coconut milk, quarter cup
- freshly cracked black pepper and salt

INSTRUCTIONS:

a) Heat the coconut oil in a pot till melted.
b) Sauté the onion in the pot for about 6 mins till it becomes translucent.
c) Include garlic and curry to the pot and cook for 2 mins till fragrant.
d) In a separate saucepan, bring chickpeas, diced tomatoes, and vegetable broth to a boil.
e) Include the chickpea mixture to the pot and cook for about 13 mins till the sauce thickens.
f) Stir in the spinach leaves and coconut milk and allow the spinach to wilt.
g) Include salt and pepper.
h) Serve with brown rice or naan bread right away.

Buddha Power Bowl

NUTRITION: Calories 460|Fat 23g grams| Saturated Fat 9g grams | Sodium 1000mg milligrams| Carbohydrates 24g grams | Protein 40g grams

INGREDIENTS:

- cooked brown rice, 1 cup
- cooked quinoa, 1 cup
- roasted sweet potatoes, 1 cup
- roasted Brussels sprouts, 1 cup
- sliced almonds, quarter cup
- olive oil, 1 tbsp
- sautéed kale, 1 cup
- chickpeas, drained and rinsed, half cup
- avocado, sliced, half
- lemon juice, 1 tbsp
- freshly cracked black pepper and salt

INSTRUCTIONS:

a) Preset the oven to 400 °F(200 degrees Celsius).
b) Slice the Brussels sprouts and sweet potatoes into bite-sized pieces.
c) On a baking sheet lined with parchment paper, drizzle olive oil over the sweet potatoes and Brussels sprouts and season them with freshly cracked black pepper and salt.
d) Roast in the preheated oven for around 25 mins, till the vegetables are soft and lightly browned.
e) While the vegetables are roasting, heat a skillet over moderate heat. Cook the kale in a tbsp of olive oil till it becomes shriveled and tender.
f) In a small bowl, combine olive oil and lemon juice to make a simple vinaigrette.
g) Divide the cooked rice and quinoa between two bowls to make the Buddha power bowl. To the bowls, include the roasted sweet potatoes, Brussels sprouts, sautéed kale, and chickpeas.
h) Drizzle the vinaigrette over the tops of every bowl, then drizzle with sliced avocado and almonds.
i) Serve right away and enjoy!

Asian Beef and Vegetable Stir-Fry

NUTRITION: Calories 296| Total Fat 16g| Saturated Fat 5.9g | Trans Fat 0.6g| Polyunsaturated Fat 1g| Monounsaturated Fat 6.4g| Cholesterol 103mg| Sodium 639mg

INGREDIENTS:

- sirloin steak, sliced into strips, 1 pound
- honey, 1 tbsp
- Minced garlic, 2 cloves
- rice vinegar, 1 tbsp
- freshly cracked black pepper and salt
- grated ginger, 1 tsp
- coconut oil, 2 tbsps
- red bell pepper, sliced, 1
- yellow onion, sliced, 1
- sliced mushrooms, 1 cup
- soy sauce, 2 tbsps
- sliced broccoli florets, 2 cups

INSTRUCTIONS:

a) Melt the coconut oil in a sizeable skillet.
b) Brown the sliced sirloin for 5 mins. Set aside.
c) Heat a skillet and cook the red bell pepper and yellow onion slices till they become tender. This should take around 6 mins.
d) Include the minced garlic to the skillet and sauté it for about 2 mins or till it becomes fragrant.
e) Include the broccoli florets and mushrooms to the skillet and continue to sauté for another 6 mins, or till they are tender.
f) Combine soy sauce, rice vinegar, honey, and grated ginger in a small bowl.
g) Combine the sauce with the beef and vegetables in the skillet. Include salt and pepper to taste.
h) Serve right away with brown rice.

Mushroom Stroganoff

NUTRITION: Calories: 167|Fat: 5g|Saturated: 1g|Carbohydrate: 23g |Fiber: 3g|Protein: 6g | Sodium: 821mg

INGREDIENTS:

- sliced mushrooms, 1 pound
- Egg noodles, cooked
- sour cream, 1 cup
- Flour,2 tbsps
- olive oil, 2 tbsps
- minced garlic, 3 cloves
- vegetable broth, 1 cup
- butter, 2 tbsps
- freshly cracked black pepper and salt
- Sliced onion, 1
- Dijon mustard, 1 tbsp

INSTRUCTIONS:

a) Heat the olive oil and butter in a big frying pan over moderate-high heat.
b) Cook the sliced mushrooms, onion, and garlic by frying them for around 6 mins till they become soft.
c) Put the flour into the frying pan and stir it well till the vegetables are completely covered.
d) Include the vegetable broth and whisk to thicken the sauce.
e) Over low heat, stir in the sour cream and Dijon mustard.
f) Include salt and pepper according to your preference.
g) Place the cooked egg noodles on top of the mushroom stroganoff.

Rice and Turkey Stuffed Bell Peppers

NUTRITION: Calories 292.5|Fat 6g|Saturated Fat 1.8 g| Sodium 798.7 mg | Potassium 634.2 mg| Carbohydrate 29.2 g| Protein 31.1 g

INGREDIENTS:

- bell peppers, tops slice off and seeds removed, 4
- cooked brown rice, 1 cup
- tomato sauce, 1 cup
- sliced fresh parsley, quarter cup
- ground turkey, 1 pound
- onion, sliced, 1
- Minced garlic, 2 cloves
- freshly cracked black pepper and salt

INSTRUCTIONS:

a) Preset the oven to 375°F.
b) Brown the ground turkey in a sizeable skillet over moderate-high heat.
c) Sauté the sliced onion and minced garlic in the same skillet till the onion is tender.
d) Combine in the cooked brown rice, tomato sauce, sliced parsley, salt, and pepper.
e) Fill the bell peppers with the mixture and place them in a baking dish.
f) Bake the stuffed bell peppers for about 30 mins or till they become tender.

Cheesy Shrimp with Zucchini Noodles

NUTRITION: Calories 12|Fat 0.3g grams| Saturated Fat 0.1g grams | Carbohydrates 0.5g grams| Fiber 0.1g grams | Sugars 0.1g grams| Protein 1.3g| Sodium 75mg

INGREDIENTS:

- red pepper flakes, quarter tsp
- olive oil, 2 tbsps
- freshly cracked black pepper and salt
- Minced garlic, 2 cloves
- shrimp, peeled and deveined, 1 pound
- zucchini, spiralized into noodles, 2
- Parmesan cheese, grated

INSTRUCTIONS:

a) Heat the olive oil in a sizeable skillet over moderate-high heat.
b) Cook garlic with red pepper flakes by sautéing them for 2 mins.
c) Include the shrimp and cook for around 3 mins or till they turn pink and fully cooked.
d) Take out the shrimp from the skillet and keep them aside.
e) Sauté the zucchini noodles for about 4 mins till they become soft.
f) drizzle with salt and pepper according to your taste.
g) Place the zucchini noodles on four dishes and top with the sautéed shrimp.
h) If preferred, drizzle with grated Parmesan cheese.

Baked Sweet Potato with Black Bean and Corn Salsa

NUTRITION: Calories 460|Fat 23g grams| Saturated Fat 9g grams | Sodium 1000mg milligrams| Carbohydrates 24g grams | Protein 40g grams

INGREDIENTS:

- olive oil, 1 tbsp
- freshly cracked black pepper and salt
- sweet potatoes, 4
- frozen corn, thawed, 1 cup
- red onion, sliced, 1
- red bell pepper, sliced, 1
- sliced fresh cilantro, quarter cup
- lime juice, 2 tbsps
- black beans, drained and rinsed, 1 can
- jalapeño pepper, seeded and minced, 1

INSTRUCTIONS:

a) Preset the oven to 400°F.
b) Clean the sweet potatoes and poke them several times with a fork.
c) Place the sweet potatoes on a baking sheet and bake for about an hour till they become tender.
d) In a sizeable bowl, combine the black beans, thawed corn, sliced red onion, diced red bell pepper, minced jalapeño pepper, sliced cilantro, lime juice, olive oil, salt, and pepper. Take the roasted sweet potatoes out of the oven and serve with the black bean and corn salsa.
e) Serve immediately.

RHYTHM SNACKS AND DESSERTS

Peanut Butter Banana Oat Bars

NUTRITION: Calories 254| Fat 37 g| Cholesterol 166 mg| Sodium 411 mg | Carbohydrates 73| Protein 41 g

INGREDIENTS:

- ripe bananas, mashed, 2
- peanut butter, half cup
- maple syrup, quarter cup
- old-fashioned rolled oats, 2 cups
- sliced peanuts, quarter cup
- Pinch of salt

INSTRUCTIONS:

a) Preset the oven to 350°F.
b) Prepare an 8x8-inch baking dish by lining it with parchment paper.
c) In a sizeable mixing dish, combine the mashed bananas, peanut butter, and maple syrup.
d) Stir in the rolled oats, sliced peanuts, and salt till completely blended.
e) Evenly distribute in the prepared baking dish.
f) Put the baking dish in the oven and bake for about 28 mins or till the mixture turns golden brown.
g) Take out the baking dish from the oven and let it cool for 10 mins before slicing it into bars.

Berry Chia Seed Pudding

NUTRITION: Calories: 363 | Fat: 29g | Carbohydrates: 22.3g | Fiber: 6.6g | Sugars: 13.4g | Protein: 11.2g|Sodium 171.6 mg

INGREDIENTS:

- almond milk, 1 cup
- honey, 1 tbsp
- fresh or frozen mixed berries, half cup
- chia seeds, 2 tbsps
- vanilla extract, half tsp

INSTRUCTIONS:

a) Blend the almond milk, mixed berries, honey, and vanilla essence till smooth.
b) Transfer the mixture to a mixing bowl and combine in the chia seeds.
c) Refrigerate the bowl for at least 30 mins, till the pudding has thickened.
d) If desired, garnish the pudding with extra fresh berries.

Baked Cinnamon Apple Chips

NUTRITION: 233 calories| protein 4.8g|carbohydrates 27.7g |dietary fiber10.1g|sugars 14.4g| fat 12.7g|saturated fat 1.1g |Sodium 83 mg

INGREDIENTS:

- 2 apples
- cinnamon, 1 tbsp
- 1 tbsp sugar (if desired)

INSTRUCTIONS:

a) Preset the oven to 225°F.
b) Prepare a baking sheet with parchment paper.
c) Using a mandolin slicer, thinly slice the apples.
d) Arrange the apple slices in a single layer on the lined baking sheet.
e) In a small bowl, combine the cinnamon and sugar.
f) Sprinkle the cinnamon sugar mixture over the apple slices.
g) Bake the apple chips for around 2half hours, or till they become crispy.
h) Let the apple chips cool down completely before serving.

Roasted Garlic Hummus

NUTRITION: 290 calories | 9g Fat | 3.5g saturated fat | 38g Carbohydrates | 7g dietary fiber | 13g protein | 25mg Sodium

INGREDIENTS:

- chickpeas, drained and rinsed, 2 cans
- Tahini, quarter cup
- olive oil, quarter cup
- Water, as needed
- lemon juice, quarter cup
- freshly cracked black pepper and salt
- roasted garlic, 2 cloves
- cumin, half tsp

INSTRUCTIONS:

a) Preset the oven to 400°F.
b) Take off the top of the garlic bulb and drizzle it with olive oil.
c) Wrap the garlic in foil and bake it for 35 mins till it becomes soft and has a pleasant aroma.
d) Using a food processor, blend the chickpeas, tahini, olive oil, lemon juice, roasted garlic cloves, cumin, salt, and pepper till it becomes smooth and creamy.
e) If the hummus is too dense, include water gradually, one tsp at a time, till the desired consistency is obtained.
f) Serve the hummus with pita chips, and veggies, or use it as a spread for sandwiches.

WEEK 5: STRIDE

Week 5 of Metabolic Flexibility focuses on incorporating exercise and movement into your daily routine to support metabolic flexibility. This week includes meals and snacks that are designed to support an active lifestyle and promote optimal recovery after exercise.

The body's capacity to effectively utilize energy during physical activity is referred to as "stride", which is another aspect of metabolic flexibility. Specific to exercise, stride refers to the balance of fat and carbohydrate metabolism. During low-energy workouts, the body uses fat as a fuel source. However, because carbohydrates can be broken down more quickly to provide muscle energy, the body begins to shift toward carbohydrate metabolism as exercise intensity increases.

Keeping a fair step during exercise is significant for advancing Metabolic flexibility, as extreme dependence on one or the other fat or sugar digestion can prompt diminished execution and expanded hazard of injury. For instance, individuals who place an excessive amount of stress on the metabolism of carbohydrates run the risk of becoming fatigued and losing endurance, while those who place an excessive amount of stress on the metabolism of fat run the risk of losing muscle mass and performing at a lower level.

Nutrition, exercise intensity, and training status are just a few of the factors that can affect stride. Consuming a reasonable eating regimen that incorporates the two carbs and fats can assist with supporting productive energy digestion during exercise. Training regimens that incorporate both low- and high-intensity exercise can also help to improve stride length and metabolic flexibility.

Sweet Potato and Egg Breakfast Skillet

NUTRITION: Calories 460|Fat 23g grams| Saturated Fat 9g grams | Sodium 1000mg milligrams| Carbohydrates 24g grams | Protein 40g grams

INGREDIENTS:

- 1 sweet potato, peeled and diced
- olive oil, 1 tbsp
- 2 eggs
- paprika, half tsp
- freshly cracked black pepper and salt
- garlic powder, half tsp
- Fresh parsley, sliced (if desired)

INSTRUCTIONS:

a) Warm up 1 tbsp of olive oil in a sizeable skillet over moderate heat.
b) Apply a mixture of paprika, garlic powder, salt, and pepper to the diced sweet potato.
c) Cook till the sweet potato is tender and slightly caramelized, stirring periodically.
d) In the sweet potato mixture, make two wells, one for every egg.
e) Cover and heat the skillet for around 4 mins, till the eggs are set.
f) Include fresh parsley as a topping, if desired.

Almond Butter and Banana Overnight Oats

NUTRITION: Calories 254| Fat 37 g| Cholesterol 166 mg| Sodium 411 mg | Carbohydrates 73| Protein 41 g

INGREDIENTS:

- unsweetened almond milk, half cup
- old-fashioned rolled oats, half cup
- almond butter, 1 tbsp
- banana, mashed, half
- vanilla extract, half tsp
- honey (if desired), 1 tsp
- sliced banana and sliced almonds, for topping

INSTRUCTIONS:

a) Whisk together the rolled oats, almond milk, almond butter, mashed banana, vanilla extract, and honey (if using) in a dish.
b) Refrigerate the bowl overnight, wrapped in plastic wrap.
c) Divide the oats between two dishes and top with sliced banana and sliced almonds in the morning.

Strawberry-Banana Smoothie Bowl

NUTRITION: Calories 260 | Protein 4.4 grams| Fat 2.9 grams |Carbohydrates 40.5 grams |Sodium 77 mg

INGREDIENTS:

- Greek yogurt, half cup
- almond milk, half cup
- 1 banana, frozen and sliced
- half cup frozen strawberries
- granola, quarter cup
- 1 tbsp chia seeds

INSTRUCTIONS:

a) Blitz the banana, strawberries, almond milk, and Greek yogurt till smooth.
b) Fill a bowl halfway with the smoothie and top with oats and chia seeds.

Cottage Cheese and Fruit Plate

NUTRITION: Calories: 161| Fat: 0.6g | Carbohydrates: 41.6g | Fiber: 5.6g | Sugars: 33.1g | Protein: 1.7g | Sodium: 8mg

INGREDIENTS:

- honey, 1 tbsp
- cottage cheese, 1 cup
- sliced walnuts, quarter cup
- mixed fresh fruit, 1 cup

INSTRUCTIONS:

a) Arrange the fruit and cottage cheese on a platter.
b) Pour honey over the dish and scatter the sliced walnuts on top.
c) Enjoy!

Chicken Broccoli Casserole

NUTRITION: Calories: 405.3|Protein: 32.2g |Carbohydrates: 3.6g |Dietary Fiber: 1.5g |Sugars: 0.1g|Fat: 29.2g |Saturated Fat: 7.8g |Cholesterol: 127.7mg|Iron: 2mg |Sodium: 177.6mg

INGREDIENTS:

- Mayonnaise, half cup
- grated cheddar cheese, half cup
- fresh broccoli florets, 4 cups
- sour cream, half cup
- condensed cream of chicken soup, 1 can
- cooked and shredded chicken, 2 cups
- freshly cracked black pepper and salt
- grated Parmesan cheese, quarter cup
- onion powder, half tsp
- garlic powder, half tsp
- cooked rice, 1 cup
- Butter for greasing the casserole dish

INSTRUCTIONS:

a) Set the oven to 375 °F(190 °F) and butter a 9-by-13-inch casserole.
b) In a sizeable dish, combine the cooked and shredded chicken, fresh broccoli florets, and cooked rice.
c) Whisk together mayonnaise, sour cream, grated cheddar cheese, grated Parmesan cheese, garlic powder, onion powder, salt, and pepper in a separate bowl till well combined and smooth.
d) Include the mixture to the chicken, broccoli, and rice mixture and stir till everything is coated evenly.
e) Place the components in a greased casserole dish in an even layer.
f) Bake for 30 mins, or till the top is golden brown and the mixture is bubbly.

Grilled Vegetable Panini

NUTRITION: Calories 160| Fat 3g (Saturated 0g) | Cholesterol 0mg | Sodium 549mg| Carbohydrate 30g| Dietary Fiber 5g | Protein 8g.

INGREDIENTS:

- eggplant, sliced into rounds, 1
- fresh mozzarella cheese, 4 slices
- olive oil, 2 tbsps
- zucchini, sliced lengthwise, 1
- balsamic vinegar, 1 tbsp
- red bell pepper, sliced into strips, 1
- Pinch salt and pepper
- yellow onion, sliced into rings, 1
- whole-grain bread, 4 slices
- Handful of fresh basil leaves

INSTRUCTIONS:

a) Preset the grill to moderate-high heat.
b) In a sizeable bowl, toss eggplant, zucchini, red bell pepper, and onion with olive oil, balsamic vinegar, salt, and pepper.
c) Grill the vegetables for 6 mins on every side till they are tender and have grill marks.
d) Allow the vegetables to cool for a few mins.

TO ASSEMBLE THE SANDWICHES

e) Layer the grilled vegetables, mozzarella cheese, and fresh basil leaves between two slices of bread.
f) Heat a panini press or grill pan over moderate-high heat.
g) Place the sandwiches on the panini press or grill pan and cook for around 4 mins on every side, or till the cheese is melted.
h) Serve immediately and enjoy!

Greek Turkey Burger

NUTRITION: Calories 292.5|Fat 6g|Saturated Fat 1.8 g|Sodium 798.7 mg |Potassium 634.2 mg|Carbohydrate 29.2 g|Protein 31.1 g

INGREDIENTS:

- ground turkey, 1 pound
- sliced red onion, quarter cup
- crumbled feta cheese, quarter cup
- Minced garlic, 2 cloves
- sliced fresh parsley, quarter cup
- freshly cracked black pepper and salt
- whole wheat buns, 4 buns
- Lettuce, 4 leaves
- Tomato, 4 slices
- Tzatziki sauce for serving

INSTRUCTIONS:

a) Heat the grill or grill pan.
b) Combine ground turkey, feta cheese, garlic, salt, parsley, red onion, and pepper in a sizeable mixing dish.
c) Make four equal-sized patties out of the mixture.
d) Grill patties for around 4 mins per side, till done.
e) Grill the buns for 2 mins.
f) Top burgers with lettuce, tomato, and tzatziki sauce.

Chicken and Peanut Lettuce Wraps

NUTRITION: Calories: 386| Fat: 11.5g | Carbohydrates: 27.4g | Fiber: 1.9g | Sugars: 24.3g | Protein: 43.6g |Sodium 174 mg

INGREDIENTS:

- ground chicken, 1 pound
- vegetable oil, 1 tbsp
- ginger, minced, 1 tbsp
- Minced garlic, 2 cloves
- Lettuce, 9 leaves
- cucumber, sliced, 1
- soy sauce, quarter cup
- honey, 1 tbsp
- sliced peanuts, quarter cup
- rice vinegar, 2 tbsps
- chili garlic sauce, 2 tbsps
- peanut butter, quarter cup
- Fresh cilantro, for garnish

INSTRUCTIONS:

a) Heat the vegetable oil in a sizeable skillet over moderate-high heat.
b) Cook the ground chicken in the skillet, stirring occasionally, for about 6 mins till it's browned and cooked through.
c) In a small bowl, combine soy sauce, rice vinegar, chili garlic sauce, honey, and peanut butter till well combined and smooth.
d) Pour the sauce over the cooked chicken in the skillet and stir to coat evenly.
e) Cook for another 2 mins, stirring occasionally, till the sauce thickens slightly.
f) Stir in the sliced peanuts and eliminate the skillet from the heat.
g) To assemble the lettuce wraps, place a small amount of the chicken mixture onto every lettuce leaf.
h) Garnish with sliced cucumber and fresh cilantro.
i) Roll the lettuce leaves up and serve right away.

Chickpea Salad Sandwich

NUTRITION: 197 Calories| Protein 7.8g| Carbohydrates 24.2g | Fiber 3.7g | sugar 3.1 g | Fat 8.3g | Saturated fat 4.3g | Sodium 233mg

INGREDIENTS:

- Dijon mustard, 1 tbsp
- lemon juice, 1 tbsp
- plain Greek yogurt, quarter cup
- chickpeas, drained and rinsed, 1 can
- freshly cracked black pepper and salt
- celery, diced, 2 stalks
- Diced onion, 1
- Bread or lettuce leaves (for serving)

INSTRUCTIONS:

a) Mash the chickpeas till they are roughly crushed.
b) Combine in the Dijon mustard, lemon juice, celery, onion, Greek yogurt, salt, and pepper.
c) Serve the chickpea salad with slices of bread or lettuce leaves.

Zucchini Noodle Soup

NUTRITION: Calories 160| Fat 3g (Saturated 0g) | Cholesterol 0mg | Sodium 549mg| Carbohydrate 30g| Dietary Fiber 5g | Protein 8g.

INGREDIENTS:

- olive oil, 1 tbsp
- vegetable broth, 4 cups
- Minced garlic, 2 cloves
- freshly cracked black pepper and salt
- Spiralized zucchinis, 2
- dried thyme, quarter tsp

INSTRUCTIONS:

a) In a pot, heat olive oil over moderate heat.
b) Include garlic to the pot and sauté for about 2 mins till fragrant.
c) Include zucchini noodles to the pot and cook for around 3 mins till they become tender.
d) Stir in vegetable broth, thyme, salt, and pepper.
e) Bring the soup to a boil, then reduce the heat and let it simmer on low for 6 mins.
f) Serve the soup immediately.

Cauliflower Fried Rice with Shrimp

NUTRITION: Calories 12|Fat 0.3g | Saturated Fat 0.1g | Carbohydrates 0.5g | Fiber 0.1g | Sugars 0.1g| Protein 1.3g| Sodium 75mg

INGREDIENTS:

- shrimp, peeled and deveined, 1 pound
- Sliced onion, 1
- Riced cauliflower, 1 head
- Minced garlic, 2 cloves
- Sliced red bell pepper, 1
- freshly cracked black pepper and salt
- soy sauce, 2 tbsps
- coconut oil, 2 tbsps

INSTRUCTIONS:

a) In a sizeable skillet set over moderate heat, melt the coconut oil.
b) Sweat the onion and bell pepper till they become soft and tender.
c) Cook the shrimp till they are pink, then include the garlic.
d) Once the riced cauliflower and soy sauce are added, continue cooking for about 6 mins.
e) Then, season with salt and pepper according to your taste.

Baked Cod with Asparagus

NUTRITION: Calories:303| Fat: 7.9g | Carbohydrates: 12.2g | Fiber: 3g | Sugars: 5.9g | Protein: 45.2g | Sodium: 329.6mg

INGREDIENTS:

- Asparagus, 1 pound
- lemon, juiced, 1
- Cod, 4 fillets
- Minced garlic, 2 cloves
- olive oil, 2 tbsps
- freshly cracked black pepper and salt

INSTRUCTIONS:

a) Preset the oven to 375°F.
b) Combine the lemon juice, salt, pepper, garlic, and olive oil in a bowl.
c) Apply the mixture onto the fish fillets.
d) Put the fillets on a baking sheet and bake for 18 mins or till the fish is thoroughly cooked.
e) After baking for 10 mins, include the asparagus to the baking sheet and combine it with the fish juices. Continue baking for 8 more mins.

Lemon and Herb Chicken Thighs with Broccoli

NUTRITION: 244 Calories| 10g Fat (2g Saturated)| 47mg Cholesterol | 314mg Sodium| 19g Carbohydrates (8g fiber| 11g Sugar | 0g Added)| 25g Protein

INGREDIENTS:

- broccoli florets, 1 pound
- sliced fresh thyme, 1 tbsp
- lemons, juiced and zested, 2
- Minced garlic, 2 cloves
- freshly cracked black pepper and salt
- Chicken, 4 thighs
- sliced fresh rosemary, 1 tbsp
- olive oil, 2 tbsps

INSTRUCTIONS:

a) Preset the oven to 375°F.
b) In a bowl, combine lemon juice, lemon zest, minced garlic, sliced thyme, sliced rosemary, and olive oil.
c) Rub the mixture all over the chicken thighs, and season with salt and pepper.
d) Bake the chicken for about 28 mins.
e) Include broccoli to the dish and toss with the chicken juices.
f) Return to the oven and bake for an additional 10 mins, or till the chicken is cooked through and the broccoli is tender.

Steak Fajitas with Peppers and Onions

NUTRITION: 280 Calories| 7g Fat (1g Saturated)| 236mg Sodium | 34g Carbohydrates (6g fiber| 5g Sugar)| 23g Protein

INGREDIENTS:

- flank steak, sliced, 1 pound
- cumin, 1 tsp
- Diced red bell pepper, 1
- sliced onion, 1
- olive oil, 2 tbsps
- chili powder, 1 tbsp
- freshly cracked black pepper and salt
- green bell pepper, diced, 1
- Tortillas for serving

INSTRUCTIONS:

a) To prepare this dish, you will need a sizeable skillet, which should be heated over high heat.
b) Once the skillet is hot, include a generous amount of olive oil and let it heat up for a few seconds.
c) Next, include the sliced beef to the skillet and stir occasionally, letting it cook for around 3 mins till it's browned on all sides.
d) After this, you should include the peppers and onion to the skillet, mixing them well with the beef.
e) Cook for an additional 4 mins, stirring occasionally till they are fully softened and cooked through.
f) Include chili powder, cumin, salt, and pepper.
g) Enjoy with tortillas.

Nut, Fruit, and Seed Trail Combine

NUTRITION: Calories: 120 | Fat: 1.9g | Carbohydrates: 28.2g | Fiber: 5.1g | Sugars: 21.6g | Protein: 2.2g | Sodium: 0mg

INGREDIENTS:

- Almonds, half cup
- pumpkin seeds, half cup
- Cashews, half cup
- dried cranberries, half cup

INSTRUCTIONS:

a) Combine all of the components.
b) Enjoy.

Banana, Cinnamon, and Oat Cookies

NUTRITION: Calories: 121| Fat: 3.2g | Carbohydrates: 17.8g | Fiber: 3g | Sugars: 2.5g | Protein: 3.9g|Sodium 95 mg

INGREDIENTS:

- 2 ripe bananas, mashed
- Rolled oats, 1 cup
- cinnamon, half tsp
- almond butter, quarter cup
- honey or maple syrup, quarter cup
- vanilla extract, 1 tsp

INSTRUCTIONS:

a) Set the oven to 350°F.
b) In a mixing dish, combine the mashed bananas, rolled oats, almond butter, sweetener, vanilla extract, and cinnamon.
c) Using a spoon, drop spoonfuls of the mixture onto a baking sheet that has been covered with parchment paper.
d) Bake for 18 mins, or till the top is golden brown.
e) Before serving, allow the cookies to cool fully.

Easy Berry Sorbet

NUTRITION: Calories: 255| Fat: 16.1g | Carbohydrates: 30.2g | Sodium: 99.4mg | Fiber: 4.4g| Sugars: 17.2g | Protein: 2.8g

INGREDIENTS:

- 2 cups frozen mixed berries
- water, quarter cup
- quarter cup honey or maple syrup

INSTRUCTIONS:

a) Blend the frozen berries, honey/maple syrup, and water in a blender till smooth.
b) Serve right away as a light dessert or snack.

WEEK 6: DOWNHILL

Week 6 of Metabolic Flexibility focuses on rest and recovery to support metabolic flexibility. This week includes meals and snacks that are designed to support a relaxed and stress-free lifestyle and promote restful sleep.

The body's ability to use energy effectively during periods of recovery and rest, such as sleep or relaxation, is referred to as "downhill." During these periods, the body shifts towards fat digestion, as it is a more productive fuel source for low-power exercises.

Because it enables the body to switch between fuel sources as needed throughout the day, efficient downhill metabolism is important for promoting metabolic flexibility. Moreover, people with effective downhill digestion might encounter further developed rest quality, higher energy levels, and less metabolic issues like weight gain and type 2 diabetes.

A few variables can impact downhill digestion, including sustenance, rest propensities, and feelings of anxiety. During times of recovery and rest, a well-balanced diet rich in healthy fats can aid in the efficient metabolism of fat. Moreover, laying out a steady rest timetable and reducing feelings of anxiety can assist with working on generally speaking Metabolic flexibility.

Smoked Salmon and Cream Cheese Bagel

NUTRITION: Calories 330 |Fat 17.7g| Cholesterol 109.1mg|Sodium 126.5mg |Carbohydrates 1g|Sugar 0g| Fiber 0.4g|Protein 39.5g

INGREDIENTS:

- whole wheat bagel, sliced and toasted, 1 bagel
- smoked salmon, 2 ounces
- cream cheese, 2 tbsps
- red onion, thinly sliced, quarter
- Capers, 1 tbsp

INSTRUCTIONS:

a) On the toasted bagel slices, spread the cream cheese.
b) Top with the smoked salmon, red onion, and capers.
c) Serve right away.

French Toast with Fresh Berries

NUTRITION: Calories: 170| 3g Fat| 171mg Sodium| 30g Carbohydrates (4g fiber| 15g Sugar| 7g Added)| 7g Protein

INGREDIENTS:

- whole grain bread, 4 slices
- unsweetened almond milk, half cup
- vanilla extract, 1 tsp
- honey, 1 tbsp
- Cinnamon, quarter tsp
- mixed berries, quarter cup
- Eggs, 2

INSTRUCTIONS:

a) Combine the eggs, almond milk, vanilla extract, and cinnamon in a bowl.
b) Dredge the slices of bread into the batter and fry them in a hot, oiled skillet till they turn golden brown.
c) Drizzle with honey or maple syrup and top with mixed berries.

Keto Breakfast Casserole

NUTRITION: Calories: 284| Fat: 19.1g | Carbohydrates: 16g | Fiber: 3.1g | Sugars: 12.5g | Protein: 12.9g|Sodium 33 mg

INGREDIENTS:

- ground breakfast sausage, 1 pound
- green bell pepper, diced, 1
- onion, diced, half
- Eggs, 8
- heavy cream, half cup
- garlic powder, half tsp
- shredded cheddar cheese, 1 cup
- onion powder, 1 tsp
- dried oregano, 1 tsp
- Pinch salt and freshly cracked black pepper
- red bell pepper, diced, 1
- sliced fresh parsley, quarter cup

INSTRUCTIONS:

a) Preset the oven to 375°F.
b) Cook the breakfast sausage in a sizeable skillet till it is fully cooked.
c) Include bell peppers and onions to the skillet and cook for about 5 mins till they become tender.
d) Combine the eggs, heavy cream, garlic powder, onion powder, dried oregano, salt, and freshly cracked black pepper in the skillet.
e) Spread the sausage and vegetable mixture evenly on the bottom of a 9x13-inch baking dish.
f) Sprinkle shredded cheddar cheese over the sausage mixture.
g) Bake for around 28 mins or till the eggs are fully cooked and the cheese is melted and bubbly.
h) If preferred, garnish with fresh parsley before serving.

Grilled Portobello Mushroom Burger

NUTRITION: Calories: 167|Fat: 5g|Saturated: 1g|Carbohydrate: 23g |Fiber: 3g|Protein: 6g | Sodium: 821mg

INGREDIENTS:

- 1 Portobello mushroom cap
- 1 whole wheat bun
- quarter avocado, mashed
- diced tomato, quarter cup
- Dijon mustard, 1 tbsp
- sliced red onion, 2 tbsps

INSTRUCTIONS:

a) Grill the Portobello mushroom cap till soft.
b) Toast the whole wheat bread. Spread the mashed avocado on the bottom bun.
c) Place the grilled Portobello mushroom cap on top of the avocado.
d) Layer the diced tomato and sliced red onion on the mushroom cap.
e) Spread the Dijon mustard on the top bun and top with the vegetables.

Lobster Roll

NUTRITION: Calories: 215 | Fat: 7 g | Saturated Fat: 1.0 g | Sodium: 128 Mg | Carbohydrate: 36 g | Dietary Fiber: 9 g | Sugar: 14 g | Protein: 7 g

INGREDIENTS:

- cooked and diced lobster meat, 4 ounces
- whole wheat hot dog bun, 1 bun
- diced celery, quarter cup
- diced red onion, quarter cup
- Mayonnaise, 1 tbsp
- lemon juice, 1 tbsp
- freshly cracked black pepper and salt

INSTRUCTIONS:

a) Combine the cooked lobster meat, diced celery, diced red onion, mayonnaise, lemon juice, salt, and pepper.
b) Serve the mixture in the whole wheat hot dog bun.

Pork and Feta Meatball Lettuce Wraps

NUTRITION: 197 calories| Protein 7.8g| carbohydrates 24.2g | dietary fiber 3.7g | sugar 3.1 g | fat 8.3g | saturated fat 4.3g | Sodium 358mg

INGREDIENTS:

- ground pork, 1 pound
- dried oregano, half tsp
- sliced fresh mint, quarter cup
- Minced garlic, 2 cloves
- crumbled feta cheese, half cup
- Juice of half lemon
- freshly cracked black pepper and salt
- sliced fresh parsley, quarter cup
- olive oil, 1 tbsp
- Butter lettuce leaves, for serving
- Tzatziki sauce, for serving

INSTRUCTIONS:

a) Set the oven to 375 °F(190 °F).
b) Combine the ground pork, feta cheese, parsley, mint, garlic, oregano, salt, pepper, and lemon juice in a sizeable mixing dish. Combine thoroughly.
c) Make small meatballs using the mixture, around 2 inches in diameter.
d) Heat the olive oil in a sizeable skillet over moderate-high heat.
e) Cook the meatballs, flipping them regularly, for around 6 mins, till they are browned.
f) Transfer the meatballs to a baking sheet and bake for around 12 mins, till they are fully cooked.
g) Wrap the meatballs in butter lettuce leaves and drizzle with tzatziki sauce to serve.

Turkey and Cranberry Sandwich

NUTRITION: Calories 292.5|Fat 6g|Saturated Fat 1.8 g|Sodium 798.7 mg |Potassium 634.2 mg|Carbohydrate 29.2 g|Protein 31.1 g

INGREDIENTS:

- whole grain bread, 2 slices
- sliced turkey breast, 4 ounces
- cranberry sauce, quarter cup
- baby spinach, quarter cup
- Mayonnaise, 1 tbsp

INSTRUCTIONS:

a) Spread the mayonnaise on one slice of bread.
b) Place the sliced turkey, cranberry sauce, and baby spinach on top of the mayonnaise.
c) Serve with the remaining slice of bread.

Chicharrónes-Crusted Pork Tenderloin

NUTRITION: Calories 421| 43g Fats| 5g Carbohydrates| 27g Protein | Sodium 98 mg

INGREDIENTS:

- pork tenderloin, 1 pound
- Almonds, half cup
- crushed chicharrónes, half cup
- garlic powder, half tsp
- smoked paprika, 1 tsp
- Egg, 1
- Sliced cauliflower, 1 head
- olive oil, 1 tbsp
- chipotle in adobo sauce, 1 tbsp
- heavy cream, quarter cup
- freshly cracked black pepper and salt

INSTRUCTIONS:

a) Set the oven to 375 °F(190 °F).
b) Blitz the almonds, chicharrónes, garlic powder, smoked paprika, salt, and pepper and put in a bowl.
c) In a separate shallow bowl, whisk the egg till well beaten.
d) Dip the pork tenderloin into the egg mixture, ensuring it is fully coated.
e) Dredge the pork in the almond mixture, pushing it to the surface to adhere.
f) In an oven-safe skillet, melt the butter.
g) Sear the pork for about 4 mins, till it is browned on all sides.
h) Transfer the pork to the oven and bake for around 18 mins, or till it reaches an internal temperature of 145°F.
i) While the pork is cooking, boil the cauliflower in a pot for around 10 mins, till it is tender.
j) Blitz the cooked cauliflower, olive oil, and chipotle in adobo sauce, heavy cream, salt, and pepper till it is smooth and creamy.
k) Serve the sliced pork tenderloin with the chipotle cauliflower smash.

Seared Scallops with Lemon Beurre Blanc

NUTRITION: Calories 668| Fat 18g (Saturated 8g) | Cholesterol 257mg | Sodium 602mg| Carbohydrate 75g| Dietary Fiber 11g | Protein 56g.

INGREDIENTS:

- 6 ounces sea scallops
- half cup white wine
- lemon juice, 2 tbsps
- 4 tbsps butter, cubed
- freshly cracked black pepper and salt

INSTRUCTIONS:

a) Sprinkle salt and pepper over the sea scallops to season them.
b) In a skillet, cook the scallops on every side for about 3 mins till they turn golden brown and are fully cooked. Set them aside.
c) In the same skillet, combine white wine and lemon juice.
d) Cook the mixture over high heat till it has reduced.
e) Low-heat the sauce, then whisk in the diced butter till it is melted and incorporated.
f) Drizzle the lemon beurre Blanc over the cooked scallops before serving.

Pan-Seared Halibut with Mango Salsa

NUTRITION: Calories: 266| Fat: 8.8g | Carbohydrates: 19.9g | Fiber: 3.7g | Sugars: 1.5 g| Protein: 29.1g | Sodium: 895.8mg

INGREDIENTS:

- halibut fillet, 6 ounces
- diced red onion, quarter cup
- freshly cracked black pepper and salt
- sliced fresh cilantro, quarter cup
- mango, diced, 1
- lime juice, 1 tbsp

INSTRUCTIONS:

a) Season the halibut fillet with salt and pepper, then proceed to cook it in a skillet over moderate-high heat.
b) Cook the halibut for about 4 mins on every side till it is fully cooked. Set it aside.
c) In a small bowl, combine the sliced mango, red onion, cilantro, lime juice, salt, and pepper, tossing them together.
d) Serve the mango salsa beside the pan-seared halibut.

Eggplant and Asparagus Rollatini with Pesto

NUTRITION: Calories: 241| Fat: 9.2g | Carbohydrates: 9.8g | Fiber: 3.7g | Sugars: 3.5 g | Protein: 30.7g | Sodium: 750mg

INGREDIENTS:

- asparagus, trimmed, 1 bunch
- grated Parmesan cheese, half cup
- Sliced eggplant, 1
- freshly cracked black pepper and salt
- ricotta cheese, half cup
- lemon juice, 1 tbsp
- Tahini, quarter cup
- crumbled feta cheese, half cup
- Minced garlic, 2 cloves
- olive oil, 2 tbsps
- pesto, quarter cup

INSTRUCTIONS:

a) Preset the oven to 375 °F (190 degrees Celsius).
b) Arrange the eggplant slices on a baking sheet lined with parchment paper.
c) Brush both sides of every slice with olive oil and drizzle with salt and pepper.
d) Bake for about 25 mins till the eggplant slices are tender. Set them aside.
e) Blanch the asparagus in boiling salted water for around 3 mins. Drain and rinse with cold water to stop the cooking process. Set the asparagus aside.
f) In a dish, combine feta cheese, ricotta cheese, grated Parmesan cheese, tahini, garlic, lemon juice, and salt and pepper to taste.
g) Place the roasted eggplant slices on a plate and spoon a generous amount of the cheese mixture on top.
h) Roll the eggplant slices into "rollatinis" by adding a couple of asparagus spears to every slice.
i) Arrange the rollatinis on a baking tray and top them with pesto.
j) Bake for around 25 mins till the cheese is melted and bubbly.
k) If preferred, top with more grated Parmesan cheese and fresh herbs.

Philly Cheese Steak and Roasted Tomato Melts

NUTRITION: Calories: 215 | Fat: 7 g | Saturated Fat: 1.0 g | Sodium: 128 Mg | Carbohydrate: 36 g | Dietary Fiber: 9 g | Sugar: 14 g | Protein: 7 g

INGREDIENTS:

- beef sirloin or ribeye, thinly sliced, 1 pound
- Sliced tomatoes, 2
- Sliced green bell pepper, 1
- Diced onion, 1
- provolone cheese, 8 slices
- garlic powder, half tsp
- freshly cracked black pepper and salt
- Bread, 8 slices
- Sliced red bell pepper, 1

INSTRUCTIONS:

a) Heat the oven to 350°F before using.
b) Prepare the beef by cooking it in a sizeable skillet till the pink color disappears. Keep it aside.
c) Using the same skillet, include the diced peppers and onions.
d) Cook while occasionally stirring till the peppers and onions become tender and acquire a slight caramelized color.
e) Include garlic powder, salt, and pepper to the mixture according to your taste. Set it aside.
f) Place the bread slices on a baking sheet in an organized manner.
g) Top every slice with a tomato slice, cooked meat, sautéed peppers and onions, and a slice of provolone cheese.
h) Put the baking sheet in the oven and bake for around 6 mins, or till the cheese has melted and begins to bubble.

Flank Steak with Charred Broccoli

NUTRITION: Calories 296| Total Fat 16g |Saturated Fat 5.9g| Trans Fat 0.6g |Polyunsaturated Fat 1g|Monounsaturated Fat 6.4g |Cholesterol 103mg |Sodium 639mg

INGREDIENTS:

- flank steak, 1 pound
- freshly cracked black pepper and salt
- canned chipotle peppers in adobo sauce, 1 tbsp
- broccoli slice into florets, 1 head
- olive oil, 1 tbsp
- lime, slice into wedges, 1
- chili powder, 1 tbsp
- unsalted butter softened, quarter cup
- smoked paprika, 1 tsp
- garlic powder, half tsp

INSTRUCTIONS:

a) Preset a grill or grill pan to a moderate-high temperature.
b) In a small bowl, combine the chili powder, smoked paprika, garlic powder, salt, and pepper.
c) Smear the spice mixture on the flank steak.
d) Combine the softened butter and sliced chipotle peppers in a separate small bowl. Set aside.
e) Toss salt and pepper with the broccoli florets and combine with olive oil.
f) Put the flank steak on the grill and grill every side for 4 mins.
g) Grill the broccoli for around 6 mins till it has a gentle browning.
h) Take the steak and broccoli off the grill and let them rest for 5 mins before slicing.
i) Serve the sliced steak with a dab of chipotle butter on the side, along with the scorched lime broccoli.
j) Before serving, squeeze the lime wedges over the broccoli and steak.

Keto Zucchini Noodle Carbonara

NUTRITION: Calories 160| Fat 3g (Saturated 0g) | Cholesterol 0mg | Sodium 549mg| Carbohydrate 30g| Dietary Fiber 5g | Protein 8g.

INGREDIENTS:

- Spiralized zucchinis, 3
- Minced garlic, 2 cloves
- grated Parmesan cheese, quarter cup
- Sliced bacon, 8 ounces
- Pinch of salt and freshly cracked black pepper
- sliced fresh parsley, 2 tbsps
- heavy cream, half cup
- egg yolks, 3

INSTRUCTIONS:

a) Preset a sizeable skillet over moderate-high heat.
b) Cook the bacon, turning it occasionally, for around 10 mins till it becomes crispy and browned.
c) Transfer the bacon to a dish covered in paper towels.
d) Whisk heavy cream, egg yolks, and freshly grated Parmesan cheese.
e) Incorporate the minced garlic into the skillet and cook for 2 mins.
f) After adding the zucchini noodles, toss them in the skillet with the garlic and bacon oil.
g) Cook the noodles for 2 to 3 mins till they become tender but still slightly firm.
h) Toss the zucchini noodles with the cream mixture after pouring it over them.
i) Cook for an additional one to two mins, allowing the noodles to be thoroughly coated and the sauce to slightly thicken.
j) Include desired amounts of parsley, salt, and freshly cracked black pepper.
k) Divide the carbonara with zucchini noodles into bowls and drizzle every serving with crispy bacon.
l) Enjoy!

Cauliflower Tots

NUTRITION: 157 calories| Protein 7.8g| carbohydrates 24.2g | dietary fiber 3.7g | sugar 3.1 g | fat 8.3g | saturated fat 4.3g |Sodium 11 mg

INGREDIENTS:

- almond flour, half cup
- grated Parmesan cheese, quarter cup
- minced garlic, 2 cloves
- dried parsley, 1 tsp
- salt, half tsp
- Egg, 1
- freshly cracked black pepper, quarter tsp
- Sliced cauliflower, 1 head
- Avocado oil or olive oil, for frying

INSTRUCTIONS:

a) Set the oven to 400°F.
b) Place the sliced cauliflower in a bowl that is safe to use in the microwave and heat it on high power for roughly 6 mins till it reaches a soft consistency. Then, set it aside.
c) Combine the egg, almond flour, Parmesan cheese, garlic, parsley, salt, and freshly cracked black pepper in a dish.
d) Take a tbsp of the mixture and shape it into small tots.
e) Line a baking sheet with parchment paper and arrange the tater tots on it.
f) Put the baking sheet with the tater tots in the oven and bake them for around 18 mins till they become golden brown and crispy.
g) On moderate-high heat, warm up avocado or olive oil in a sizeable skillet.
h) Cook the tots in the heated oil for about 3 mins on every side.
i) If preferred, top the cauliflower tots with more Parmesan cheese and sliced parsley.

Blueberry and Lemon Scones

NUTRITION: Calories: 470| Fat: 35.4g | Carbohydrates: 26.8g | Fiber: 8.1g | Sugars: 11g | Protein: 12.6g | Sodium: 367mg

INGREDIENTS:

- all-purpose flour, 1¾ cups
- fresh blueberries, half cup
- lemon zest, 1 tbsp
- salt, quarter tsp
- unsalted butter, cubed, half cup
- granulated sugar, quarter cup
- baking powder, 2half tsps
- heavy cream, ⅓ cup

INSTRUCTIONS:

a) Set the oven to 400 °F.
b) In a bowl, combine the flour, sugar, baking soda, and salt.
c) Include the butter to the mixture and blend it in till the texture becomes similar to coarse crumbs.
d) Include blueberries and lemon zest.
e) Include heavy cream gradually while stirring regularly till it forms a dough.
f) Slice the dough into wedges after forming it into a round on a floured board.
g) Bake for around 20 mins till browned.

Lemon Ricotta Cookies

NUTRITION: 290 calories | 9g Fat | 3.5g saturated fat | 38g Carbohydrates | 7g dietary fiber | 13g protein | 25mg Sodium

INGREDIENTS:

- lemon juice, 2 tbsps
- softened butter, half cup
- Egg, 1
- ricotta cheese, 1 cup
- granulated sugar, 1 cup
- baking powder, 1 tsp
- flour, 2 cups
- lemon zest, 1 tbsp
- baking soda, half tsp
- salt, quarter tsp

INSTRUCTIONS:

a) Preset the oven to 375°F.
b) In a bowl, combine the flour, baking powder, baking soda, and salt.
c) In a separate bowl, cream the butter and sugar together till they become light and fluffy.
d) Include the egg, ricotta cheese, lemon juice, and zest to the butter and sugar mixture.
e) Gradually stir in the dry components till the mixture forms a dough-like consistency.
f) Drop tbsps of the dough onto a baking sheet lined with parchment paper and bake for around 14 mins or till they turn golden brown.

EXERCISE AND METABOLIC FLEXIBILITY

There are a few activities that can assist with advancing Metabolic flexibility, including:

HIIT

HIIT, which stands for High-Intensity Interval Training, involves engaging in short bursts of vigorous physical activity followed by periods of rest or low-intensity exercise. This form of training has been demonstrated to promote metabolic flexibility by enhancing mitochondrial synthesis and insulin sensitivity. HIIT has been shown in studies to enhance metabolic flexibility in both healthy persons and those with metabolic diseases such as type 2 diabetes.

HIIT offers the advantage of being time-efficient, making it a convenient option for individuals with busy schedules. It can be performed using various types of exercises, including cycling, running, or bodyweight movements like burpees and jumping jacks. However, before beginning any new exercise program, consult with a healthcare professional, especially if you have any underlying health conditions or are new to exercise.

Resistance Training

By increasing muscle mass and enhancing insulin sensitivity, resistance training, such as weight lifting, can assist in promoting metabolic flexibility. Additionally, this type of training may aid in fat loss and overall body composition improvement. Resistance training has been found in studies to increase metabolic flexibility in both healthy persons and those with metabolic diseases such as obesity and type 2 diabetes.

Resistance training is also good for keeping muscle mass, which is vital for general metabolic health. Muscle tissue is metabolically active, which means it consumes calories even when not in use.

Weights, resistance bands, or bodyweight movements such as push-ups, squats, and lunges can be used to include resistance training to your exercise program. It is critical to collaborate with a healthcare expert or qualified personal trainer who can assist you in developing a resistance training program that is both safe and effective. This program can be customized to suit your requirements and align with your desired fitness goals.

Low-Intensity Exercise

By increasing fat metabolism and insulin sensitivity, low-intensity exercise, such as walking or cycling at a moderate pace, can aid in metabolic flexibility. People who are just starting an exercise program or may have health conditions that prevent them from engaging in high-intensity exercise can benefit most from this type of exercise. Low-intensity exercise can aid in fat oxidation and mitochondrial activity, both of which are significant elements in metabolic flexibility. Furthermore, low-intensity exercise is often less stressful on the body than high-intensity exercise, which can be advantageous for people who are dealing with health issues or injuries.

You can integrate low-intensity exercise into your routine by strolling, yoga, swimming, or moderate cycling. It is crucial to engage in a minimum of 150 mins of moderate-intensity physical activity or 75 mins of vigorous-intensity exercise every week. This can be done in small sessions of 13 mins every throughout the week.

Pilates and yoga

By reducing stress and increasing insulin sensitivity, yoga, and Pilates can assist in promoting metabolic flexibility. These kinds of exercises are especially good for people who might not be able to exercise at a high intensity because of health issues or physical limitations.

Yoga has been proven to improve metabolic function and insulin sensitivity, two key aspects of metabolic flexibility. Pilates, on the other hand, has been found to increase metabolic function and promote weight loss, both of which can contribute to improved metabolic flexibility.

Attending a class in a studio or gym, or following along with an online video or app, are two ways to incorporate yoga or Pilates into your routine. It is critical to select a class or video that is appropriate for your skill level and fitness objectives. It is also critical to listen to your body and alter or skip exercises that are too difficult or uncomfortable.

CONCLUSION

To summarize, metabolic flexibility is critical for sustaining optimal health and wellness. You may improve your body's ability to transition between using different energy sources and boost general health by implementing the recipes and advice in "The Complete Metabolic Flexibility Cookbook" into your daily routine. Before implementing significant alterations to your diet or exercise regimen, it is advisable to consult with a healthcare professional. We hope you enjoy these tasty and nutritious dishes and take the first step toward metabolic flexibility.

Recap of the benefits of metabolic flexibility

When our body is in a state of metabolic flexibility, it can seamlessly switch between using different fuel sources to meet its energy needs, like carbohydrates and fats. There are numerous advantages to this ability for both performance and overall health. First and foremost, metabolic flexibility ensures daylong energy levels that are stable and consistent. By effectively exchanging between fuel sources, people with metabolic flexibility experience diminished energy plunges and further developed efficiency.

Furthermore, optimal weight management relies heavily on metabolic flexibility. The body can keep a healthy balance between how much energy it uses and how much it takes in thanks to its adaptive use of carbohydrates and fats as fuel. This flexibility aids in weight loss or maintenance by preventing excessive fat storage and encouraging efficient fat burning.

Moreover, blood sugar regulation is affected by metabolic flexibility. The body's ability to switch between carbohydrates and fats effectively lowers the risk of insulin resistance and type 2 diabetes by stabilizing blood glucose levels. Additionally, this metabolic flexibility improves insulin sensitivity, which is crucial for optimal metabolic health as a whole.

Metabolic flexibility has also been linked to enhanced endurance and physical performance. The ability to use a variety of fuel sources at varying intensities of activity is advantageous for regular exercisers and athletes. With this flexibility, stored fat can be used more effectively during low-intensity workouts and carbohydrates can be used more effectively during high-intensity workouts.

Finally, metabolic flexibility may have a beneficial effect on longevity and aging. According to the findings of the research, maintaining metabolic flexibility can assist in reversing the age-related decline in energy metabolism, which in turn can promote overall longevity and healthy aging.

In synopsis, metabolic flexibility offers a scope of advantages including supported energy levels, ideal weight for the executives, further developed glucose guidelines, improved actual execution, and possible consequences for maturing and life span. Metabolic flexibility promotes overall health and well-being by encouraging the effective utilization of various fuel sources.

Steps to take for optimal metabolic flexibility

To upgrade and keep up with ideal metabolic flexibility, there are a few stages you can take. The most important steps to increase metabolic flexibility are as follows:

Healthy Diet

Embrace a fair eating routine that incorporates different supplements and thick food sources. Whole foods like fruits, vegetables, lean proteins, whole grains, and healthy fats should be your primary focus. Reduce your intake of refined and processed foods, added sugars, and unhealthy fats.

Managing Carbohydrates

While carbs are a significant energy source, dealing with their admission can advance metabolic flexibility. Maintain a moderate carbohydrate intake and put vegetables and whole grains, which are rich in complex carbohydrates, ahead of refined ones. This supports fat utilization and aids in avoiding excessive insulin spikes.

Wholesome fats

Remember wellsprings of solid fats for your eating regimens, like avocados, nuts, seeds, greasy fish, and olive oil. By providing an alternative source of fuel and enhancing satiety, these fats encourage metabolic flexibility.

Fasting intermittently

You might want to think about adding intermittent fasting to your routine. Fasting and eating times are alternated during this eating pattern. By encouraging the body to use stored fat for energy during the fasting period, it can improve metabolic flexibility.

Regular sport
Regular physical activity that incorporates strength training and aerobic exercise is recommended. This blend further develops insulin responsiveness, advances fat usage, and improves general metabolic capability.

HIIT
Make high-intensity interval training a part of your workout routine. Short bursts of intense exercise are followed by rest or low-intensity activity in HIIT. It has been demonstrated to increase fat-burning and metabolic flexibility by enhancing mitochondrial function.

Quality sleep
To support metabolic health, prioritize quality sleep. The absence of rest can upset the hormonal equilibrium and lead to insulin obstruction, influencing metabolic flexibility. Each night, aim for 7-9 hours of uninterrupted sleep.

Stress Reduction
To reduce long-term stress, try stress management methods like deep breathing exercises, meditation, or hobbies. Metabolic flexibility can be negatively impacted by high levels of stress.

Normal Dinner Timing
Lay out normal dinner timings and stay away from delayed times of fasting or inordinate nibbling. Steady dinner designs assist with directing insulin and improve metabolic capability.

Individualized Methodology
Keep in mind that different people may have different levels of metabolic flexibility. Listening to your body, keeping track of how different diet and lifestyle changes affect you, and getting personalized advice from a doctor or registered dietitian are all important.

You can support and enhance your metabolic flexibility, thereby enhancing your overall health and well-being, if you follow these steps and live a healthy lifestyle.

Future Directions

The idea of metabolic flexibility is still the subject of a lot of research, and scientists are looking into a lot of interesting new directions for the future. Several possibilities for investigation include:

Strategies for the diet

Specific dietary interventions' effects on metabolic flexibility are the subject of research. For instance, investigate how metabolic flexibility and overall health are affected by various macronutrient ratios, such as diets high in fat or low in carbohydrates. Furthermore, investigating the impacts of explicit supplements, for example, polyphenols or omega-3 unsaturated fats, on metabolic flexibility is an intriguing area of study.

Exercise and Preparing

An important step in the right direction is to gain a deeper comprehension of how various training strategies and exercise modalities affect metabolic flexibility. This includes determining the ideal exercise type, intensity, and duration for promoting metabolic flexibility in a variety of populations, including athletes, people with metabolic disorders, and elderly people.

Epigenetic and genetic influences

The genetic and epigenetic factors that influence metabolic flexibility are the subject of research. Examining the job of explicit qualities, hereditary varieties, and epigenetic adjustments in metabolic flexibility might help in recognizing people who are more inclined toward metabolic resoluteness and creating customized mediations.

Stomach Microbiota

It has become clear that the microbiota in the gut could play a role in metabolic health and flexibility. A future examination might zero in on figuring out the perplexing cooperations between stomach microorganisms, digestion, and metabolic flexibility. It is possible to increase metabolic flexibility by manipulating the gut microbiota through diet, prebiotics, probiotics, or fecal microbiota transplantation.

Diseases of the liver

One important direction for the future is to investigate the role of metabolic flexibility in the onset and progression of metabolic disorders like obesity, type 2 diabetes, and cardiovascular diseases. There may be significant clinical implications for comprehending the underlying mechanisms and investigating therapeutic interventions to enhance metabolic flexibility in these conditions.

Assessment and biomarkers

An area of interest is the creation of biomarkers for metabolic flexibility that are dependable and easily accessible. Early detection, personalized interventions, and monitoring of treatment outcomes could all benefit from the identification of specific metabolic markers or signatures that indicate metabolic flexibility or rigidity.

Maturing and Life span

An intriguing direction is to investigate how metabolic flexibility affects aging and longevity. Strategies for healthy aging could be developed by examining the role of metabolic flexibility in age-related metabolic decline, cellular senescence, and diseases.

These new directions have the potential to improve our comprehension of metabolic flexibility and its effects on human health. Targeted interventions and individualized approaches to enhance metabolic flexibility and overall metabolic health may emerge from ongoing research in these areas.

30-DAY MEAL PLAN

Day	BREAKFAST	LUNCH	DINNER	SNACK/DESSERT
WEEK 1				
1	Keto Pancakes	Pork Chops with Romesco Butter and Broccoli	Eggplant and Asparagus Rollatini with Pesto	Avocado Egg Boat
2	Bacon Egg Cups	Chicken Broccoli Casserole	Baked Cod with Asparagus	Coconut Chia Pudding
3	Blueberry Almond Protein Smoothie	Buddha Power Bowl	Chicharrónes-Crusted Pork Tenderloin	Chocolate Banana Ice Cream
4	Chive and Gruyère Frittata with Crab and Bacon	Broiled salmon with quinoa and roasted vegetables	Enchilada Bowl	Blueberry Oat Bars
5	Strawberry-Banana Smoothie Bowl	Low-Carb Burger Bowl	Roasted Cauliflower Steaks with Zucchini	Baked Sweet Potato Fries
6	Banana Nut Muffins	Salmon Avocado Power Bowl	Rice and Turkey Stuffed Bell Peppers	Coconut Macaroons
7	Oatmeal with nuts and seeds	Cashew, and Asparagus Stir-Fry with Cauliflower Rice	Mushrooms and Fresh Tomato Salad	Apple Crisp
WEEK 2				
8	Spinach and feta omelet	Asian Beef and Vegetable Stir-Fry	Roasted Miso Salmon with Green Beans	Cinnamon Roasted Almonds
9	Berry Nut Butter Smoothie	Chicken and Peanut Lettuce Wraps	Roasted Cauliflower Steaks with Zucchini	Lurnea coconut Log
10	Cheesy Breakfast frittata	Deconstructed Egg Roll	Philly Cheese Steak and Roasted Tomato Melts	Bacon-Stuffed Avocados
11	Zucchini, and Pepper Jack Quiche	Sweet Potato and Black Bean Bowl	Beef Veggie Stew	Cauliflower Tots
12	Bacon Egg Cups	Shrimp and Avocado Salad	Lentil Veggie Soup	Apple Chips
13	Salmon and Avocado Toast	Chicken Skewers with Carrot and Walnut Salad	Spaghetti squash with meat sauce	Nut, Fruit, and Seed Trail Combine

14	Smoked Salmon and Cream Cheese Bagel	Stuffed Chicken Breasts with Balsamic Kale	Mushroom Stroganoff	Peanut Butter and Jelly Energy Bites
WEEK 3				
15	Greek Yogurt Breakfast Parfait	Greek Turkey Burger	Pan-Seared Halibut with Mango Salsa	Lemon Ricotta Cookies
16	Blueberry Almond Protein Smoothie	Turkey and Hummus Wrap	Shrimp, and fennel stew	Mixed Berry Cobbler
17	Keto Breakfast Casserole	Deconstructed Egg Roll	Baked salmon with asparagus and lemon	Simple Egg Salad
18	Shakshuka	Chickpea Salad Sandwich	Keto Zucchini Noodle Carbonara	Ham, Cheese, and Egg Rolls
19	Cottage Cheese and Fruit Plate	Broiled Salmon with Asparagus	Turkey chili	Chocolate Avocado Puddin
20	Green Smoothie Bowl	Chickpea and Spinach Curry	Grilled steak with roasted sweet potatoes	Chocolate Chip Banana Bread
21	Breakfast quinoa bowl	Philly Cheese Steak Bowl	Seared Scallops with Lemon Beurre Blanc	Chocolate Zucchini Bread
WEEK 4				
22	Banana Nut Muffins	Coconut Chicken	Steak Fajitas with Peppers and Onions	Berry Chia Seed Pudding
23	French Toast with Fresh Berries	Lobster Roll	Cauliflower Crust Pizza	Chocolate Peanut Butter Energy Bites
24	Keto Breakfast Casserole	Broccoli Cheddar Soup	Beef Veggie Stew	Cauliflower Tots
25	Breakfast burrito	Zucchini Noodle Soup	Spicy Shrimp and Zucchini Noodles	Blueberry and Lemon Scones
26	Cottage Cheese and Fruit Plate	Black bean and Sweet potato tacos	Grilled pork chops with roasted vegetables	Baked Sweet Potato Fries
27	Sweet Potato and Egg Breakfast Skillet	Mediterranean Quinoa Salad	Baked Cod with Asparagus	Easy Berry Sorbet
28	Breakfast Burrito Bowl	Mediterranean Tuna Bowl	Mushroom Stroganoff	Blueberry Oat Bars
WEEK 5				
29	Bacon and Veggie Frittata	Grilled Portobello Mushroom Burger	Grilled shrimp and vegetable kebabs	Chocolate Zucchini Bread
30	Banana pancakes	Tuna salad sandwich	Turkey chili	Roasted Garlic Hummus

MEASUREMENTS CONVERSION CHART

TO CONVERT X » Y	1 OF THIS	EQUALS THIS
VOLUME TO WEIGHT		
tbsps » tsps	1 tbsp	3 tsps
tbsps » fluid ounces	1 tbsp	0.5 fluid ounces
tbsps » sticks of butter	1 tbsp	0.125 sticks
tbsps » cups	1 tbsp	0.0625 cups
tsps » tbsps	1 tsp	0.33 tbsps
tsps » cups	1 tsp	0.02 cups
tsps » fluid ounces	1 tsp	0.16 fluid ounces
fluid ounces » tbsps	1 fluid ounce	2 tbsps
fluid ounces » tsps	1 fluid ounce	6 tsps
fluid ounces » cups	1 fluid ounce	0.125 cups
cups » fluid ounces	1 cup	8 fluid ounces
cups » tbsps	1 cup	16 tbsps
cups » tsps	1 cup	48 tsps
cups » pints	1 cup	0.5 pints
cups » quarts	1 cup	0.25 quarts
cups » gallons	1 cup	0.0625 gallons
pints » cups	1 pint	2 cups
quarts » pints	1 quart	2 pints
quarts » cups	1 quart	4 cups
gallon » quarts	1 gallon	4 quarts
gallon » cups	1 gallon	16 cups
pinch » tsps	1 pinch	0.1 tsps
dash » tsps	1 dash	0.2 tsps
cup dry beans » pounds	1 cup dry beans	0.4 pounds
cup butter » pounds	1 cup butter	0.5 pounds
cup choc. chips » ounces	1 cup chocolate chips	6 ounces
cup cheerios » ounces	1 cup cheerios	1.33 ounces
cup cocoa » ounces	1 cup cocoa	3 ounces
cup corn syrup » ounces	1 cup corn syrup	11.5 ounces
cup cornmeal » ounces	1 cup cornmeal	4.5 ounces
cup flour » ounces	1 cup flour	4 ounces
cup flour » pounds	1 cup flour	0.25 pounds
cup honey » pounds	1 cup honey	0.75 pounds
cup honey » ounces	1 cup honey	12 ounces
cup jam » ounces	1 cup jam	12 ounces

cup molasses » ounces	1 cup molasses	11.6 ounces
cup oats » ounces	1 cup oats	3.5 ounces
cup oats » pounds	1 cup oats	0.22 pounds
cup oil » ounces	1 cup oil	7.5 ounces
cup peanut butter » ounces	1 cup peanut butter	9.5 ounces
cup raisins » ounces	1 cup raisins	5.5 ounces
cup rice » ounces	1 cup rice	7 ounces
cup rice » pounds	1 cup rice	0.4375 pounds
cup rice flour » ounces	1 cup rice flour	4.5 ounces
cup shortening » ounces	1 cup shortening	7 ounces
cup sour cream » ounces	1 cup sour cream	8 ounces
cup sugar » ounces	1 cup sugar	7 ounces
cup sugar » pounds	1 cup sugar	0.4375 pounds
cup sugar (brown) » ounces	1 cup brown sugar	7.5 ounces
cup sugar (powdered) » ounces	1 cup powdered sugar	4 ounces
cup water » ounces	1 cup water	8.3 ounces
cup walnuts (sliced) » ounces	1 cup walnuts	4.3 ounces
cup wheat » pounds	1 cup wheat	0.48 pounds
cup dried milk (nonfat) » ounces	1 cup dried milk (nonfat)	3 ounces
egg (powdered) » ounces	1 egg (powdered)	0.5 ounces
egg (sizeable) » fluid ounces	1 egg (sizeable)	2 fluid ounces
egg white » tsps	1 egg white	8 tsps
egg white » cups	1 egg white	48 cups
egg yolk » tsps	1 egg yolk	4 tsps
stick butter » cups	1 stick butter	0.5 cups
stick butter » ounces	1 stick butter	4 ounces
stick butter » tbsps	1 stick butter	8 tbsps
tbsps baking soda » ounces	1 tbsp baking soda	0.5 ounces
tbsps baking powder » ounces	1 tbsp baking powder	0.5 ounces
tbsps baking powder » pounds	1 tbsp baking powder	0.03125 pounds
tbsps cocoa » ounces	1 tbsp cocoa	0.1875 ounces
tbsps cocoa » pounds	1 tbsp cocoa	0.01 pounds
tbsps cornstarch » ounces	1 tbsp cornstarch	0.33 ounces
tbsps jam » ounces	1 tbsp jam	0.75 ounces
tbsps honey » ounces	honey, 1 tbsp	0.75 ounces
tbsps honey » pounds	honey, 1 tbsp	0.0468 pounds
tbsps oil » ounces	1 tbsp oil	0.46875 ounces
tbsps peanut butter » ounces	1 tbsp peanut butter	0.59375 ounces
tbsps salt » ounces	1 tbsp salt	0.6 ounces
tbsps shortening » ounces	1 tbsp shortening	0.4375 ounces

tbsps spices » ounces	1 tbsp spices	0.25 ounces
tbsps vinegar » ounces	1 tbsp vinegar	0.5 ounces
tbsps yeast » ounces	1 tbsp yeast	0.5 ounces
tbsps yeast » ounces	1 tbsp yeast	0.33 ounces
tsps baking soda » ounces	1 tsp baking soda	0.16 ounces
tsps baking powder » ounces	1 tsp baking powder	0.16 ounces
tsps salt » ounces	1 tsp salt	0.2 ounces
pound flour » cups	1 pound flour	4 cups
pound sugar » cups	1 pound sugar	2.285 cups
ounces oats » cups	1-ounce oats	0.285 cups
Pound rice » cups	1 pound rice	2.285 cups
ounces salt » tsps	1-ounce salt	5 tsps
ounces jam » tbsps	1-ounce jam	1.33 tbsps
MASS TO WEIGHT		
ounce » pounds	1 ounce	0.0625 pounds
ounce » grams	1 ounce	28.35 grams
pounds » ounces	1 pound	16 ounces
pounds » kg	1 pound	0.45kg
kg » pounds	1 kg	2.2 pounds
grams » ounces	1 gram	0.035ounces
ENGLISH TO METRIC		
cup (U.S.) » mL	1 cup (U.S.)	236.58 mL
cup (U.K.) » mL	1 cup (U.K.)	284 mL
cup (Australia) » mL	1 cup (Australia)	250 mL
gallon (US) » L	1 gallon (US)	3.785 L
quart (US) » L	1 quart (US)	0.946 L
pint (US) » L	1 pint (US)	0.47 L
fluid ounces (US) » mL	1 fluid ounce (US)	29.57mL
tbsps (US) » mL	1 tbsp (US)	14.78 mL
tsps (US) » mL	1 tsp (US)	4.9285 mL
mL » cc	1 mL	1 cc

INDEX

Q

R

S

T

Z

Made in the USA
Middletown, DE
04 September 2023

37961055R00077